The Joy of Lean

Also available from ASQ Quality Press:

Kaizen Kanban: A Visual Facilitation Approach to Create Prioritized Project Pipelines
Fabrice Bouchereau

The Lean Handbook: A Guide to the Bronze Certification Body of Knowledge
Anthony Manos and Chad Vincent, editors

Executing Lean Improvements: A Practical Guide with Real-World Healthcare Case Studies
Dennis R. Delisle

Lean Doctors: A Bold and Practical Guide to Using Lean Principles to Transform Healthcare Systems, One Doctor at a Time
Aneesh Suneja and Carolyn Suneja

Making Change in Complex Organizations
George K. Strodtbeck III

The Quality Toolbox, Second Edition
Nancy R. Tague

Root Cause Analysis: Simplified Tools and Techniques, Second Edition
Bjørn Andersen and Tom Fagerhaug

The Certified Six Sigma Green Belt Handbook, Second Edition
Roderick A. Munro, Govindarajan Ramu, and Daniel J. Zrymiak

The Certified Manager of Quality/Organizational Excellence Handbook, Fourth Edition
Russell T. Westcott, editor

The Certified Six Sigma Black Belt Handbook, Third Edition
T.M. Kubiak and Donald W. Benbow

The ASQ Auditing Handbook, Fourth Edition
J.P. Russell, editor

The ASQ Quality Improvement Pocket Guide: Basic History, Concepts, Tools, and Relationships
Grace L. Duffy, editor

To request a complimentary catalog of ASQ Quality Press publications, call 800-248-1946, or visit our Web site at http://www.asq.org/quality-press.

The Joy of Lean

Transforming, Leading, and Sustaining a Culture of Engaged Team Performance

Dodd Starbird

ASQ Quality Press
Milwaukee, Wisconsin

American Society for Quality, Quality Press, Milwaukee, WI 53203
© 2016 by ASQ
All rights reserved. Published 2016.
Printed in the United States of America.

21 20 19   5 4 3

Library of Congress Cataloging-in-Publication Data

Names: Starbird, Dodd, author.
Title: The joy of lean : transforming, leading, and sustaining a culture of
   engaged team performance / Dodd Starbird.
Description: Milwaukee, Wisconsin : ASQ Quality Press, 2016. | Includes
   bibliographical references and index.
Identifiers: LCCN 2016041968 | ISBN 9780873899420 (hardcover : alk. paper)
Subjects: LCSH: Teams in the workplace--Management. | Quality
   control--Management. | Organizational effectiveness--Management. |
   Leadership.
Classification: LCC HD66 .S723 2016 | DDC 658.4/013—dc23
LC record available at https://lccn.loc.gov/2016041968

No part of this book may be reproduced in any form or by any means, electronic, mechanical, photocopying, recording, or otherwise, without the prior written permission of the publisher.

Director of Knowledge Products: Seiche Sanders
Associate Publisher: Matt T. Meinholz
Managing Editor: Paul Daniel O'Mara
Sr. Creative Services Specialist: Randall Benson

ASQ Mission: The American Society for Quality advances individual, organizational, and community excellence worldwide through learning, quality improvement, and knowledge exchange.

Attention Bookstores, Wholesalers, Schools, and Corporations: ASQ Quality Press books, video, audio, and software are available at quantity discounts with bulk purchases for business, educational, or instructional use. For information, please contact ASQ Quality Press at 800-248-1946, or write to ASQ Quality Press, P.O. Box 3005, Milwaukee, WI 53201-3005.

To place orders or to request ASQ membership information, call 800-248-1946. Visit our Web site at www.asq.org/quality-press.

∞ Printed on acid-free paper

Quality Press
600 N. Plankinton Ave.
Milwaukee, WI 53203-2914
E-mail: authors@asq.org
The Global Voice of Quality®

Dedication

This book is dedicated to everyone I've encountered on the path to improve organizational performance over the last three decades. While I've included a number of their stories here, there are also a number of other, unnamed contributors who helped to form the ideas herein. I'm grateful to every one of them for the experiences that they've given me and my team along the journey.

*While they sometimes learn from us,
we learn from them every day.*

Contents

List of Figures xi

Acknowledgements xiii

Prologue – A Lean Parable: Efficiency is the Best Form of Job Security! xv

Introduction   Lean Culture and Engaged Team Performance 1
                A Short History of Process and
                    Performance Improvement 3
                Purposeful Culture Design 5
                Engagement Defined 6
                The Power of Teams 8
                The Grand Paradox of an Efficient Culture 10
                Lean Culture by the Steps 11
                Lean Leadership 12

Chapter 1   **Find Your Purpose: Commit to Change** 13
                Why Change? Why not! 14
                First, Find Your Purpose 15
                A Vision of Perfection 18
                The Frozen Middle 19
                A Moment of Truth 20
                It Takes Leadership 21
                Moving Forward with a Purpose 22
                Leadership with a Purpose 22

Chapter 2	**Identify Opportunity: Measure and Analyze the Process**	**23**
	The Need for Change	23
	The Commitment	23
	The Path to Improvement	23
	The Transition	24
	Results	24
	Do We Really Need a Time Study?	25
	The Time Study	26
	Time Study Results	32
	Back to Quality	37
	Quality Today	38
	Quality Principles for the Future	39
	Leading as You Measure and Analyze the Process ...	40
Chapter 3	**Drive Value: Streamline the Process**	**43**
	EZB	43
	The Spirit of Lean	48
	Crappy Handoffs	50
	5S: Workplace Organization	51
	The Opportunity Matrix	52
	Flex Work in a Call Center	54
	Flex Work and Priority Protection	55
	Contact Center Pressure	55
	Leading Lean Process Streamlining	57
Chapter 4	**Control the Process: Make the Work and Data Visible**	**59**
	Visual Work and Data	59
	Collaborative Norms	62
	Rolling Whiteboards Are Expensive!	64
	Trend Charts	65
	Freedom Through Tyranny	66
	Leading Visual Data and Integrating the Next Steps	67
Chapter 5	**Transform: Organize the Team**	**69**
	A Functional Organization	69
	Customer-Focused Teams	71
	Launching the Pilots	73

	Pilot Results	74
	Organizing the Whole Department	75
	Leading the Transformation: Organize the Team	77
Chapter 6	**Engage! Set Team Goals**	**81**
	The Team's Mission	81
	Mission 24	82
	Productivity Goals	84
	Individual Goals	85
	A New Way of Measuring Productivity	87
	Stealing Work	93
	Changing Negative Culture to Positive	94
	Leading Team Goal-Setting	95
Chapter 7	**Implement Change: Lead the Transition**	**97**
	The Uphill Battle	97
	A Downhill Battle	98
	Rebellion or Revolution?	100
	Revolution	101
	Circles and Triangles	101
	Leading Engagement in Change	102
Chapter 8	**Stand The Test of Time: Sustain Lean Engaged Team Performance**	**105**
	Process-Only Focus Leads to Failure	105
	Culture Crash	106
	Resourcing a Sustainable Transformation	108
	Expanding the Lean Culture	112
	Strategy Deployment and Leader Standard Work	112
	Sustaining Strategy Deployment	115
	Leading and Sustaining Lean Culture	116
Chapter 9	**Conclusion: New Lean Tools and a New Lean Culture**	**119**
	A Lean Culture of Value Innovation	122
	A Value Innovation Strategy	123
	The Future of Lean Culture and Engaged Team Performance	126

Appendix A	A History of Process and Performance Improvement	129
	Early Ideas	130
	The Early and Mid-Twentieth Century	132
	Sociotechnical Systems............................	133
	Another Successful Team Model—W. L. Gore	134
	Kaizen, WorkOut, and Reengineering...............	134
	Lean and Six Sigma................................	135
	Centering the Pendulum	136
	Engaged Team Performance, Menlo, and Holacracy	137
	Summary	138
Appendix B	The Joy of Agile Product Development at Menlo Innovations	141
	Agile	141
	Agile Principles...................................	142
	Leading to Joy: A Purposeful Culture	145

Inspirational Sources 147

Index 149

List of Figures

Figure 1	A Lean Culture of Engaged Team Performance	3
Figure 2	Data management team's definition of *perfect*	19
Figure 3	Time study basic template	27
Figure 4	Individual time study sheet example	28
Figure 5	Client management task time	33
Figure 6	Standard time for tasks	34
Figure 7	Performance efficiency by team	36
Figure 8	Account closure payment current-state process	45
Figure 9	Future-state account closure payment process	47
Figure 10	Opportunity Matrix example	53
Figure 11	Call center priority protection	56
Figure 12	Example team whiteboard on Day 1	60
Figure 13	Turnaround time estimation	62
Figure 14	Available and completed work trended over time	66
Figure 15	Ecova energy data management process	70
Figure 16	Ecova customer-focused team whiteboard	73
Figure 17	Principal Annuities daily whiteboard	83
Figure 18	Percent of work completed in 24 hours	83
Figure 19	Bank Operations Team efficiency chart	89
Figure 20	Bank operations team efficiency improvement	91
Figure 21	The Battle of Gettysburg	99
Figure 22	General approach to strategy deployment	114
Figure 23	Strategy deployment planning at Ecova	114
Figure 24	A Lean Culture of Engaged Team Performance	120
Figure 25	Strategy Canvas of Cirque du Soleil, from *Blue Ocean Strategy*	124

Figure 26	Hierarchy of employee engagement at Assumption Life	126
Figure 27	Pendulum swings in business theory	129
Figure 28	Agile sprint cycle	144

Acknowledgements

As we proceed you'll often see the words "we and us" instead of "I and me" in the stories and explanations. Everything we do is a team effort, and so I have only a very few memories that are truly mine alone. That said, I do have a few more-personal thanks to give:

- To Jana Schmidt, Martin Sieh, David Cline, Jennifer Wilson, and Lauren Kirkley from Ecova Inc., for sharing great examples throughout their journey in revolutionizing their company's culture and performance;
- To Fred Moll, Dan Bradford, David Styka, David Mintz, my good friend David Schummers, and the Hansen Integration team at Auris Surgical Robotics, for living the ideal of an engaged team;
- To Art Bacci at Principal Financial, who gave me a wonderful learning opportunity to lead a Lean Engaged Team Performance effort from start to finish in his organization, with an inspirational purpose of improving performance for their customers;
- To Steve Whitty, Jodi Murphy, Doug Fick, Amy Friedrich, Lacy Larson, Joe McCarty, and Mark Spencer at Principal Financial, for helping the stories from our common history to come alive;
- To countless other friends at Principal Financial, GuideOne, Delta Dental, Joppa, and other organizations in Des Moines, Iowa, who helped me start my own journey in Engaged Team Performance over a decade ago and have co-presented their results with me dozens of times through the years—I'm afraid to name some because I owe so much to so many, and so I hope you all know how much I appreciate every one of you;
- To Matt Meinholz, Paul O'Mara, Janet Sorensen, Randy Benson, and the team at Quality Press, as well as peer reviewers Kaiwen Cheng, George Raub III, and Barry Bickley for their streamlined process, insightful advice, and highly professional production experience;

- To all of the team members at Implementation Partners LLC, especially including Martha Szylberg for her candid and comprehensive input on the book's content, Deirdre Gengenbach for her continuous development of great new opportunities to build our team's experiences, and our CFO, Teri Montz, who keeps the company running when I'm preoccupied with book-writing;
- To Beth Rothwell, who occasionally sends me a great new idea or book to read, many of which have ended up quoted here;
- To Drew Locher, who helped me explain some of my stories better and consistently align them with a positive vision of Lean culture;
- To David Marquet, for sharing his vision for leadership of engaged teams;
- To Rich Sheridan, for his partnership and leadership by superb example in inspiring organizations to revolutionize their cultures, and to the team at Menlo Innovations for achieving and sharing their Joy;
- To my children, James, Aspen, Autumn, and Jade, for their interested support;
- And finally, to my wife Celeste, for being the ultimate partner by balancing me, energizing me, and driving me forward.

Prologue – A Lean Parable: Efficiency is the Best Form of Job Security!

Has your organization tried Lean already? If so, you surely see and feel the Joy of Lean in your workplace now, right?

Don't worry. If you're not quite to joy yet, you're not alone.

As it attracts more and more attention as a successful business philosophy that can improve results in any type of organization, Lean has still sometimes been misunderstood as a method for just cutting expenses. The useful ideas of eliminating waste and driving greater efficiency can pick up a negative spin associated with perceptions of job cuts, employees doing more with less, and managers squeezing more productivity from each person. None of that sounds very joyful.

But it doesn't have to be that way. This book will show you how to cultivate a positive Lean Culture of excellence that creates value for customers, profitable growth for businesses, sustainable cost reduction, and fulfilling jobs for employees. As we proceed, we'll continually demonstrate how leadership plays a critical role in establishing and sustaining a Lean Culture.

In 2010 we introduced a story in the book *Building Engaged Team Performance* about a team that dramatically improved its efficiency, and we will start this book with a parable based on that story and other similar events.

A Parable of Lean Culture

Together a service department's Lean Engaged Team Performance project team used a time study to find some significant process and performance opportunities, then redesigned their process and organization with a gain of over 40% labor efficiency. After implementing process and organization structure changes, their leader developed a positive and long-term vision for using special projects and assignments in the short term, along with planned attrition over a longer time period, to reduce the team to the right size for the workload that the time study data predicted. Over 18 months, the team shed dozens of positions without any layoffs, reducing the department's budget by more than $1 million annually.

The leader demanded high performance, expecting her teams to keep up with the workflow, but she also empowered the team members to make decisions on everyday work. She engaged them in planning and balancing their time and resources to get their daily workload done. She encouraged them to connect with their customers and deliver what the customers needed and wanted. Over time, they reduced staffing while actually improving customer service. After accomplishing that dramatic reduction in staff without a single involuntary departure, the department ran well for a while. And in addition to the great results in reducing overall cost for the business, employee satisfaction increased too. It was a great place to work.

And then the economy tanked.

The company started the process of staff reductions, but this time they planned the "cut off your arm to lose weight" layoff. You know, the one where every department cuts the same percentage of people all at once, with the secret list of victims that's vetted by the leaders and their Human Resources partners and then announced in those "some of you go to this room and everyone else goes to that room" meetings. Yikes.

But when the divisional leadership asked for the cuts from her department, the leader had a different response. She was concerned about her staff, but she was also confident in her numbers. She explained, "We're already efficient. We've cut more than 40% of our staff over the last two years while maintaining the same volume. We have time study data-based models showing that if we cut more staff now, we'll immediately have to do overtime to compensate. That will just increase our costs by 50% over anything we saved!" Overtime work, of course, results in a 1.5x labor rate per hour for hourly workers.

The leader also told her boss, "But actually, with the current processes and controls we've put in place to engage the team, there's one person we don't need."

"Who's that?" he asked.

"Me."

There were no cuts from that department. Everyone stayed, including the leader. By demanding excellence and expecting efficiency from her team, she had saved them all.

When you implement Lean to create a purposeful culture of engagement, your Lean Culture will become a sustainable source of exceptional results:

Lean Culture means empowerment.

Lean Culture means better value for the customer.

Lean Culture means better performance for the organization.

Lean Culture means a more engaging, rewarding, and yes, even joyful role for each employee.

And Lean Culture provides the competitive advantages that a team needs to survive and grow.

We call the approach Lean Engaged Team Performance (Lean ETP), and it's much more than just streamlining processes. It's a purposeful combination of value innovation, process excellence, performance measures, team goals, collaborative norms, organizational structure, enabling technology, and most of all, visionary leadership. It's hard to achieve and even harder to sustain, but it's worth the journey!

Introduction: Lean Culture and Engaged Team Performance

It started on the back of a napkin.

In *Building Engaged Team Performance*, we introduced the idea of combining world-class process improvement approaches such as Lean and Six Sigma with the performance improvement concepts of High-Performing Teams in a more purposeful way. We illustrated the approach through a 2006 case study that started as a good Lean Six Sigma project and ended in a fantastically successful Lean Culture of Engaged Team Performance. The back-of-the-napkin math showed an unbelievably high opportunity for the Group Proposal Services (GPS) department at Principal Financial, which the team then actualized through a purposeful combination of process and culture.

That was the point where we realized we were on to something, but over time we learned that we needed greater emphasis on one simple ingredient: the *criticality of leadership* in creating an intentional culture of excellence.

For 10 years we have replicated that effort and led similar initiatives in other places, and we have seen a variety of outcomes; almost all were good but only some were sustainably excellent. Somewhat predictably, the key differentiator was visionary leadership: a leader who decided to create a *culture* of excellence rather than trying to simply achieve fleeting *process* excellence. While many, many companies have deployed Lean in some form, most have failed to achieve the cultural benefits that Toyota achieved when James Womack and Daniel Jones described them in their groundbreaking book, *Lean Thinking*. Many deployments have been project based and process focused without leading to a sustainable breakthrough in culture.

In 2007, *Industry Week* conducted a market survey of Lean and claimed that only 2% of responding companies believed that their Lean program was achieving its intended results. The article, entitled "Everybody's Jumping on the Lean Bandwagon, But Many Are Being Taken for a Ride," exposed a lack of progress that seemed to be mostly cultural (http://www.industryweek.com/articles/everybodys_jumping_on_the_lean_bandwagon_but_many_are_being_taken_for_a_ride_15881.aspx). The Lean process hadn't failed, but the companies had never achieved a Lean Culture. The author, Rick Pay, said:

> *Through my experience consulting with a variety of companies implementing Lean, I've learned there are [some] major reasons that companies fail to achieve benefits:*
>
> 1. *Senior management is not committed to and/or doesn't understand the real impact of Lean.*
>
> 2. *Senior management is unwilling to accept that cultural change is often required for Lean to be a success.*
>
> 3. *The company lacks the right people in the right positions.*

Quite obviously, all of the above failure modes are leadership responsibilities.

Confirming the *Industry Week* research in "Why Lean Programs Fail," Jeffrey Liker and Mike Rother cited research from the Shingo Prize committee, a leading source for evaluating the success of Lean programs, which recently surveyed past winners of their elite award and found that many had failed to sustain the processes that had enabled them to win. The survey resulted in some substantial changes to their award criteria to focus on longer-term results (http://www.lean.org/Search/Documents/352.pdf).

Of course, most purveyors of Lean recognize the cultural components and have attempted to integrate activities that help the culture grow. Often those look like training: simulation-based events for executives, yellow belt training in Lean Six Sigma for project participants, green belt certification requirements for leaders, and web-based modules to orient all employees in the process improvement tools. While these training components are key communication and development tools that create knowledge and capability in the team, culture transformation is much more than communication.

Sheep Dip Training Doesn't Change Culture!

As we'll see as we proceed, culture change comes from purposefully changing everything together—processes, customer focus, collaborative norms, measures, organization, goals, technology, skill, capabilities, and most of all, leadership. Training is a part of that effort, but it's only an enabler of a greater strategy. That greater strategy is illustrated in Figure 1.

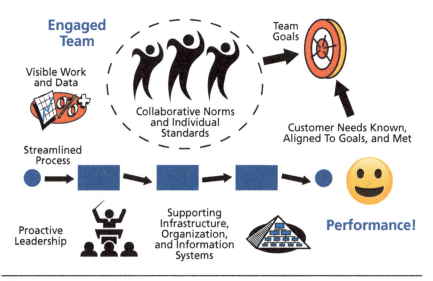

Figure 1 A Lean Culture of Engaged Team Performance.

A Lean Culture of Engaged Team Performance aligns processes, measures, goals, norms, standards, and organization with customer needs. In order to attain and sustain that alignment, you have to be willing to purposefully change all of those things in concert.

The Joy of Lean will highlight the differences between good Lean Process and great Lean Culture, illustrating how Lean done right can lead to a powerful competitive advantage. As Peter Drucker famously said, "Culture eats strategy for breakfast."

A SHORT HISTORY OF PROCESS AND PERFORMANCE IMPROVEMENT

Lean has already proven itself to be a world-changing business philosophy. Developed by Toyota over the greater part of a century, popularized by consultants such as Womack and Jones in the last three decades, and then integrated with Six Sigma in the last 15 years, the approach is credited with savings in the billions of dollars at many individual companies. The total savings across the globe could approach the size of the economies of some industrialized nations.

It's not necessary to go into a full lesson on the principles and history of Lean here.* Suffice it to say that almost everyone has seen evidence of the gains that the Lean approach has brought, either in media examples or within their own organizations.

We'll cover many of the Lean concepts as we go through the steps to transform an organization toward a Lean Culture. But we will ask you to do something now: go run a quick Internet search on Lean. You'll find many websites and articles about "elimination of waste" (starting with a really good one from the Lean Enterprise Institute that Jim Womack founded), as well as other information about the ways that the Lean tools and principles have evolved from their roots in operational tactics to focus more on non-manufacturing "transactional and service" processes today. But not one of them starts with a truly holistic description of a Lean Culture of Engaged Team Performance.

Wikipedia, while not necessarily the most reputable source for academic research, is probably the most-used quick reference tool today, and the Wikipedia page on Lean (https://en.wikipedia.org/wiki/Lean_manufacturing) somewhat unwittingly summarizes the problem for us pretty clearly:

> *For many, Lean is the set of "tools" that assist in the identification and steady elimination of waste.*

Elimination of waste is the core theme of Lean and the root source of its name, of course. And the eight wastes we're seeking to remove are a fairly well-known and comprehensive list of opportunities that came from manufacturing but now have been applied to every kind of organization:

- Transportation – Moving people, products, or information from one location to another
- Inventory – Storing products or documentation; backlog of work in process
- Motion – Movement within a work cell; movement of a mouse inside a computer
- Waiting – Waiting for parts, information, instructions, tools, tasks, or work to arrive
- Over-production – Making more than is required by the customer
- Over-processing – Doing more work or effort than the customer requires

---

See Appendix A for a more complete history of process improvement, Lean, Six Sigma, Quality, and High-Performing Teams, adapted from Chapter 2 of Building Engaged Team Performance.

- Defects – Errors, rework, scrap, or incorrect documentation
- Skills – Under-utilized human capabilities

Nevertheless, while it's true that Lean tools help organizations eliminate waste, those tools don't on their own share a vision, create a culture of teamwork and collaboration, or even sustain their own gains. Of course, the consulting companies promoting the focus on process improvement know about Toyota's strong employee engagement and the other benefits of their corporate culture of excellence, but the approach to Lean that's been spread across the world has simply emphasized process improvement instead of striking the right balance between process streamlining and team performance improvement.

We would like to nominate a ninth waste: *Failure to sustain elimination of the other eight wastes by ingraining Lean into a Culture of Engaged Team Performance!*

Although it's not always discussed in the same breath as Lean, a culture of employee engagement has become the Holy Grail of human resources programs the world over, and we have all heard of companies such as Southwest Airlines and Zappos.com that leverage their cultures to dominate their industry niches. Likewise, some of those may be missing the process and waste elimination tools that Lean would provide.

Most organizations today have strategic goals with some kind of objective for engaging their employees. But when we look deeper at companies that are trying to further those goals, we sometimes don't see a Southwest or a Zappos.com in the making. Instead of an organization designed around its culture, we often see an employee engagement "program" or initiative. Engagement should be a way of life, not a program.

You have to design your organization purposefully to foster engagement, and we will demonstrate that Lean can become a vehicle for engaging employees in transforming their processes and their culture.

PURPOSEFUL CULTURE DESIGN

Menlo Innovations, a software company, is a great example of a culture completely designed for its organization. Described by CEO Rich Sheridan in his 2013 book, *Joy, Inc.*, Menlo embodies the vision of an engaged team, which Sheridan describes as "joyful" in terms of the products they deliver for customers.

> *Joy is designing and building something that actually sees the light of day and is enjoyably used and widely adopted by the people for whom it was intended… Our mission, which we take very seriously, is to "end human suffering in the world as it relates to technology."*

Menlo is completely Lean, with an amazing culture intentionally built from the ground up. I've worked with Sheridan on presenting our approaches together at conferences, and I've been to the Menlo Innovations facility in Ann Arbor, Michigan. The place is amazing. As far as I've seen, Menlo is unique, but as we proceed in later chapters, we'll compare Menlo's approach and culture to an evolved form that incorporates Agile Development and Lean Engaged Team Performance, combined and tailored perfectly for a software development environment.*

The key enabler of the culture at Menlo was the fact that the founders designed their processes, measures, collaborative norms, and culture into the company from the very beginning. Many organizations today have to change a culture that already exists.

As Sheridan says, "Getting to simple is almost never easy."

ENGAGEMENT DEFINED

While Sheridan extolls the *business value of joy*, the opposite effect could be called the *cost of poor culture*. Although the full impact of poor culture may not be easy to measure precisely, you can probably tell which way it's moving, and you can probably identify engagement (or lack thereof) when you see it.

Christopher Mulligan, CEO of TalentKeepers, Inc., defines an engaged employee as "one who freely gives discretionary effort" and finds that engaged employees are easier to retain. Based on data found in their annual survey, Mulligan says, "People do care about money, but we find that it takes 20% more pay to get an engaged employee to leave, rather than 5% for everyone else."

Rachelle Gagnon of Assumption Life, the second-largest mutual insurance company in Canada, adds, "Engagement is a combination of three things: what employees *say*, whether employees *stay*, and how employees *strive*." She defines *striving* as the employees' willingness to apply discretionary effort for the benefit of the organization.

Employee engagement and employee appeasement are not the same thing. We've all seen the human resources engagement programs that listen to employee ideas without really enabling employees to change their own processes, then give away gift cards or award parking spaces to the employee of the month. While those efforts are certainly well-intentioned and can deliver some incremental value, they don't drive sustainable engagement. They simply recognize or reward the subset of employees who are *already* engaged.

---

* *See Appendix B for a description of Agile that highlights Menlo Innovations' unique approach, which combines Lean and team engagement principles in a product development environment.*

A friend of mine, who'll stay unnamed for her own protection, experienced that at her company, too:

> *We went through a phase where empowerment was the new thing. We had been a very top-down culture where only a few people at the top made decisions. Now managers were telling people they were empowered, but they weren't given parameters for making decisions. Very quickly, empowerment became a joke.*
>
> *I see Lean as real empowerment. When I work with leaders to set up a Lean event, I tell them we should set clear parameters for the group to make decisions, so the leader should be able to go away and come back for the report out(s) and be okay with the outcomes. Then the group is empowered to remove waste and create a process that works without having to run every suggestion up the chain of command. They feel they own the outcomes, and they are proud of their accomplishments. Once their ideas have been implemented, they can point to tangible outcomes and say, "We did that!"*

David Marquet expands upon my friend's profound assertion in his wonderful book on leadership, *Turn the Ship Around!*

> *"The problem with empowerment programs is that they contain an inherent contradiction between the message and the method. While the message is 'empowerment,' the method—it takes me to empower you—fundamentally disempowers employees."* The cultural problem is just as challenging for leaders as it is for employees, he explains. *"A recent survey reported that 44 percent of business leaders reported their disappointment in the performance results of their employees. This vexation within both parties in the workplace has one root cause: our present leadership model, which is a painfully outdated one."*

Marquet demonstrates how leaders must intentionally create an empowered culture by turning their followers into leaders, and he shows how that is possible only by returning both authority and accountability to them.

Engagement certainly doesn't come from rewards. And while recognition is an important driver in employee satisfaction, it, too, is only part of the puzzle; in order to be recognized, the employee first has to do something good. A leadership model where "it takes me to recognize you" could be disempowering as well, so modern behavioral safety programs, for example, allow *anyone* to recognize *anyone else*. Marquet clarifies:

> "*Recognizing helpful* behavior *is a necessary function of leadership, and it's a slightly different take than recognizing people. Recognizing behavior is useful and doesn't contain the inherent contradiction that the typical 'empowerment' speech contains. People feel valued when they have the ability to contribute something positive that someone else notices.*"

Engagement happens when *everyone* on the team *wants* to do something good and feels truly *empowered* to do those good things all the time. By letting people participate in positive change, Lean can become a vehicle for transferring the ownership for engagement from leaders to employees, and that will drive the discretionary effort that Christopher Mulligan and Rachelle Gagnon were talking about. And as we'll continue to demonstrate, great engagement thrives with great leadership.

THE POWER OF TEAMS

We find that engagement most often coincides with membership in a great team. People will do things for their teams that they wouldn't do for themselves. On a great team, everyone cares about each other. Everyone understands the organization's purpose and buys in to the vision.

There are certainly many great team moments in sports history, and the competition and nationalism surrounding the Olympics can set the stage for greatness. While everyone probably has a favorite "miracle moment" from hockey or basketball, one of the best examples of teamwork comes from a sport where the team might not be such an obvious component: gymnastics.

In the 1996 Atlanta Summer Olympics, the U.S. Women's Gymnastics team was leading late in the competition, with two gymnasts left to compete on the vault. Vaulting is a strenuous and difficult individual exercise; the competitor has to run toward the apparatus, hit a handspring into a springboard, flip to push off with her hands on the vault, and then complete a combination of flips, turns, and spins to land on her feet on a pad on the other side. Each gymnast gets two vault attempts.

The U.S. gymnasts were among the best in the world, and they were expected to seal the victory. Kerri Strug, the last U.S. competitor, was left to clean up the round after her teammate fell twice. Kerri's first vault was a disaster. Not only did she fall, but she landed awkwardly and stood up to find out she had damaged her ankle.

She knew she was badly hurt, and she asked her coach, the legendary Bela Karolyi, "Do we need this?" He told her that they needed her to go one more time. She limped back to the starting line, encouraged by her coach and team.

She would later learn that the ankle was severely sprained with tendon damage. After seeing her limp back to the line, nobody is sure to this day how she was able to attempt the next vault, working up to a full run, and nobody is sure how she landed that next vault on one foot. I'm confident it's not something she had ever practiced, and I'd bet you'll never see it again in an Olympic competition. Take a look at the video clip: https://www.youtube.com/watch?v=7ZRYiOa5lM8.

The U.S. team won the gold medal and ironically didn't even need Strug's vault to win, after another country's gymnast later made some errors on a floor exercise. But Strug and her team thought she needed that attempt at the time, and she landed a miracle vault on one leg when she probably should have just withdrawn from the competition.

Strug then collapsed to the floor and had to be carried to the medal ceremony. She withdrew from the individual events later in the week, giving her spot to another team member. And she returned home with her only medal from that Olympics, a team gold. She had won a team bronze medal four years before in Barcelona, and to this day she's one of the best U.S. gymnasts to have never won an individual medal in international competition.

> *The lesson: People will do things for their teams that they wouldn't think of attempting to do for themselves.*

Organizations work best when individuals identify with their teams and have a team goal of winning. Team members feel confident that the team will support them, and in return they give their best efforts, putting the team's goals ahead of their own.

In a world that increasingly celebrates individual successes, the power of a great team can get lost in translation. Whether a herd of antelope, gymnasts, or insurance quote producers, a good team can nurture and protect the individuals within it.

THE GRAND PARADOX OF AN EFFICIENT CULTURE

Efficiency gains are becoming more and more expected nowadays. As technology and process improvement techniques proliferate across the globe, efficient work is counterbalancing the benefits of cheaper labor. Believe it or not, off-shoring labor to other countries isn't quite as productive as it used to be. All organizations are becoming better at doing more with less.

Think about how it might feel to implement efficiency improvements, particularly the kinds that impact organizational design and jobs. While these kinds of projects can produce astounding results on the business side, we also know there's often an underlying fear that those efficiency improvements might hurt people by putting them out of work.

But that's not really how it has to happen.

First of all, efficiency improvement shouldn't necessarily mean reduction in staffing. Quite often the organization can find a way to use the additional capacity to drive growth. In the past when we found opportunities to cut costs by reducing staff, almost every one of those situations was handled through attrition. The vast majority of those companies consolidated open positions or moved people to other roles without a layoff; the few exceptions to this approach addressed known performance issues of specific individuals. Leaders saw the value of accomplishing those changes in a positive way so that they didn't prevent the next round of changes in the future. They didn't want to create fear of change. So while we can't promise that all future staff reductions will be handled perfectly, our history has shown that positive changes are more sustainable than negative ones.

More importantly, though, there are lots of positive implications for employees when organizations become more efficient. A number of positive benefits of Lean Engaged Team Performance boost team morale, including greater ownership and "line of sight" from their work to the customer. Most of all we know that greater efficiency vastly improves job security. Just as the insurance quoting parable in the Prologue illustrated, an efficient team is easier to protect because it pays for itself.

The Grand Paradox of an Efficient Culture is that improving processes and performance can result in humanely accomplished attrition and slower hiring in the short term, while efficiency will drive greater job security for everyone in the long term. That's all good. And so even though employees sometimes feel a little bit of fear and loathing when we start a Lean transformation, we find that they have much higher job satisfaction, morale, and job security in the end.

In a recent article, "How Going Lean Saved These Companies" (thebusinesspost.ca, 2015), Bob Tetford, the general manager and co-owner of Restwell Mattresses, credited Lean with saving the Canadian company.

They have done two waves of Lean transformation, redesigning their work together with their employees. Tetford explained:

> *Did we make a pile of money after that? No, but it has allowed us to survive. There has been a tremendous amount of change. Wages have at least doubled since we started this transformation... If we had stayed the way we were, we wouldn't be here now, not even close.*

LEAN CULTURE BY THE STEPS

This will sound like a circular argument, but the best way to integrate Lean process tools with Lean Culture is to simply engage all of the people in the organization in the transformation!

The steps to achieve a transformation to a Lean Culture of Engaged Team Performance are the same ones we outlined in *Building Engaged Team Performance* almost a decade ago:

1. *Commit to change.* Find your inspirational purpose and build a platform for change.
2. *Measure and analyze the process.* Investigate the current process and customer requirements, and measure outcomes and work standards.
3. *Streamline the work.* Improve the flow of the process to deliver value efficiently.
4. *Make the work and data visible.* Make the new work processes, collaborative norms, and control measures visually obvious in the workplace.
5. *Organize the team.* Reorganize and right-size the team for the work.
6. *Set team goals.* Assess team performance and establish team goals.
7. *Lead the transition.* Visionary leadership must invest in the culture, developing the skills, tools, systems, and knowledge to move the team to the envisioned future state.
8. *Sustain Engaged Team Performance.* Demonstrate performance over time.

A leader of a small team can use this transformational approach, or a CEO can deploy it across her entire organization. *The key is to get the entire team to participate in the transformation.*

Regardless of the scale of the change, it's critically important to communicate the approach transparently and to engage the entire organization in following the steps together. The whole team needs to understand where they are heading and why the journey is so important.

LEAN LEADERSHIP

We'll end each chapter with ideas about leadership and questions that highlight the opportunities that leaders will need to find in order to lead differently.

In her book, *Mindset*, Carol Dweck differentiates the two types of mental outlook that lead to vastly different results in business, education, and relationships. She explains that *fixed-mindset* people see their own and others' potential as mostly a function of innate talent that they don't control, while *growth-mindset* people believe that any skill can be learned or improved. While that concept sounds obvious, ask yourself if you're a great leader, artist, salesperson, and mathematician. Most people who are not named Leonardo da Vinci will invariably say that they're not good at one of those. But Dweck presents evidence that all of those skills can be learned. If you believe her thesis, it won't surprise you to hear that Leonardo da Vinci's greatest talent was probably not one of the above skills, but the passion for learning new things.

Why do we bring up that concept now? First, if you haven't read *Mindset* you probably should. That book changed the way I talk to my children even before I had finished reading it. If you intend to finish reading *this* book now and save that one for later, you need to accept the premise that *you can improve your ability to transform, lead, and sustain a culture of excellence*. If you're willing to believe that, please read on.

Here are a few questions to help you start the journey:

1. Has your organization tried Lean yet? If so, compare your approach and your results. Are you just removing waste from the process or trying to revolutionize your culture? Are you optimizing or sub-optimizing your deployment?

2. Do you see joy at work? What would be the *business value of joy* for your organization?

3. Do you need to change your culture? If so, do you really *want* to change?

As we proceed, we'll highlight the steps in transforming your organization to a Lean Culture of Engaged Team Performance, and we'll illustrate those steps both with personal stories and business examples. You'll see that a Lean Culture isn't so impossible to achieve, as long as you set out to do it purposefully.

1
Find Your Purpose: Commit to Change

In late 2014, Jana Schmidt took the reigns as CEO of Ecova Inc., a leader in energy management services. Her charge was clear: build a company capable of meeting very ambitious financial goals year after year.

Luckily, in her previous role as leader of Sales and Operations for the company, Schmidt had already launched an organizational transformation including implementation of Lean Engaged Team Performance initiatives in some key divisions (we'll explain more of the details of those efforts as we proceed). But even as the team was heading in the right direction and some results were already coming in, she knew that there was more work to do.

Schmidt explains:

> *When I joined Ecova, I was immediately attracted to the entrepreneurial spirit and the way the team would rise up to solve any challenge that came our way. But what I also saw was a lot of fire-fighting and dealing with issues that were created by solving problems in a one-off manner, rather than getting to the root cause and improving the process forever. For a young growth company, the self-discipline of engaged team performance and a commitment to process improvement do not initially sound too joyful. But all we needed was one team to try. And when that team went through the process, a key leader exclaimed that she had come to realize that we could not have built the process in a worse way. The pain her team was feeling became more clear when the end-to-end processes were mapped out.*

In her first month as CEO, she convened a transformative discussion to align the company's strategy with its financial plan, engaging all mid-level and senior leaders in assessment of the current initiatives and reprioritization of projects. Some key executives' projects were cancelled, and other new efforts were fast-tracked to launch early the next year. In a single month, they turned their priorities on a dime.

They invested in employee-led projects called "Cost Action Teams" to cut costs, trained leaders in continuous process improvement techniques called "Kaizen," and held leaders accountable for finishing ongoing implementations of "Lean Engaged Team Performance" efforts in operational areas, all the while maintaining their ongoing investments in client service improvement and international growth.

Every person in the organization was somehow involved in the changes that occurred.

Schmidt articulates her vision for Ecova's culture:

> We want to create a culture where employees can thrive in line with our values of collaboration, agility, responsibility, and passion. Our employees love energy and sustainability and want to be the best at driving down cost and consumption, and doing that in a consistent, repeatable, and high quality way enables Ecova team members to focus on consulting with clients vs. fixing problems.

Consequently, in 2015 Schmidt's team achieved their ambitious financial plan, positioning the company for an international growth push the next year. We'll return to this story over the following chapters to share more detail on how they actually accomplished these changes.

WHY CHANGE? WHY NOT!

As the famous line from a rehabilitation program goes, "The first step is admitting you have a problem." But what if you don't really have a problem?

Not everyone has a clear mandate for change, or perhaps a previous rationale for change has dissipated now that things have started going better. You shouldn't have to find your back to a wall before deciding that you want to change.

Clearly aligning your purpose with your organization's customers can help build commitment for change when there isn't yet a burning platform.

"The height of success is when you break your business, that is what I say! Just when you think things are really really going well, that's the time to change," said Ed Zander, former CEO of Motorola, in 2006. And then Motorola rode the RAZR into the ground as Apple, Palm, RIM, and others reinvented the phone.

The hardest decision to change may come when your business is also your personal brand. In order to change, you have to lose everything. Consider a musician...

Darius Rucker reinvented himself in 2008. At one time the front-man of the rock band Hootie and the Blowfish and then off to a new adventure as a country singer, Rucker found that the cue for his transformation was simply in following his passion for music. He won the 2009 Country Music Association (CMA) New Artist of the Year award, and his cover of "Wagon Wheel" in 2013 took him to the pinnacle of his new genre. Fittingly, "Wagon Wheel" is about a man hitchhiking south to Raleigh, North Carolina, to start a new life. In early 2014, Rucker won the Grammy Award for Best Country Solo Performance at the 56th Annual Grammy Awards.

Rucker's reinvention as a country music artist carried some considerable risk, of course. Rucker's Grammy win makes him only the second African American (the other was Charley Pride) to win a vocal performance Grammy award in a country music category

Change is not just for musicians! If Hootie can change, why can't we? (By the way, most people don't know that Rucker didn't really go by the name 'Hootie'—the band was named for two other people.)

FIRST, FIND YOUR PURPOSE

The mandate of being a new CEO is a strong reason for change, but not everyone has that kind of opportunity for clarity, and the rationale for change can dissipate ("when things are really really going well," as Ed Zander said above) as the burning platform's flames die out and become embers over time. And a financial goal may not translate into a shared vision for all employees. You don't need a burning platform if you can find an inspirational purpose.

First you have to find your purpose. We could mean that on many levels, of course, from a personal purpose to an organizational one. The combination of those purposes has come to be called a North Star, which Prasad Kaipa describes as *the highest aspiration that ignites both my natural genius and that of my organization.* People crave that kind of aligned purpose, and great leaders find a way to inspire a common purpose in every person in their organizations. We find that the best purpose is connected to a customer need rather than an internal aspiration.

Some organizations have a clearer purpose than others. Drew Locher, author of *Lean Office and Service Simplified*, says in a recent newsletter that there has to be an *inspirational* purpose:

> *How can an organization connect with not just the 'hands' of its associates—their physical abilities—but their 'heads and hearts,' their ideas for improvement of the business? Consider volunteer organizations. Why would an individual contribute uncompensated time…? How can that same spirit be translated to for-profit, for-pay organizations? Most importantly, such organizations have an inspirational purpose that volunteers share.*

A non-profit called Joppa serves the homeless community in Des Moines, Iowa, helping with food, clothing, and fuel in the cold winters, all while trying to enable homeless people to get into more sustainable solutions for permanent housing. Their mission sounds like something important that everyone could support:

> *To create a community of unconditional love, support and hope for the homeless, as we work together to end homelessness in Central Iowa.*

A purpose can't be any clearer than Joppa's; Joppa helps homeless people survive, get into housing, and rebuild their lives.

On the other hand, a financially-focused business purpose might not ring so clearly as a call to action for your teams:

> *To create a consistent trend of earnings and volume growth so that our stock price will go up, and we can eventually be acquired by a bigger company so that our executives and shareholders can make a shipload of money.*

That one probably won't motivate most of the team to go above and beyond the call of duty.

While making money may be some of the reason that your organization is in business, of course, a closer connection to your customers may help you find your real purpose. Employees feel a greater connection to their work when they have a better understanding of customers' needs and expectations, and when they know the score of the game, both from an external (customer) and internal (financial) standpoint. They aren't quite as motivated, however, to "beat the competition" or "meet our financial plan" as they are to "change the world" for customers.

The business that I lead certainly needs to provide a living for our team members in order to sustain itself, but we also see a greater purpose:

> *Implementation Partners LLC exists to inspire every leader to transform the cultures of their organizations and deliver exceptional business results by developing efficient and effective processes and giving every employee a chance to contribute their best work on an engaged, sustainable, winning team.*

We want to change the world to make it more efficient and effective, which will lift everyone's standard of living while creating rewarding, valued roles for every employee. That feels like an important purpose to our team members.

Roche, the medical device and pharmaceutical company, has posted a strong purpose statement on its website:

> **Doing now what patients need next**
>
> *We believe it's urgent to deliver medical solutions right now—even as we develop innovations for the future. We are passionate about transforming patients' lives. We are courageous in both decision and action. And we believe that good business means a better world.*
>
> *That is why we come to work each day. We commit ourselves to scientific rigor, unassailable ethics, and access to medical innovations for all. We do this today to build a better tomorrow.*
>
> *We are proud of who we are, what we do, and how we do it. We are many, working as one across functions, across companies, and across the world.*
>
> **We are Roche.**

And there's not a word there about beating competitors or making money.

Regardless of what words you choose, however, the most important thing about a mission or a purpose statement is to develop it *together*. Whether the words ring perfectly true or not, the employees of an organization won't want to see them brought down from a mountain by the leadership team and presented with the words already etched into stone tablets. That's only worked once in history. Find a way to engage your whole team in the writing and revision process, and refresh it occasionally.

A VISION OF PERFECTION

One tool that we find quite useful to engage a whole team in a Lean transformation effort is a "Vision of Perfection" discussion. We haven't seen that one described in other books or materials, but it's so simple that it seems impossible that we invented it. Nevertheless, we find that it's a very effective way to lead a powerful conversation to define "perfect" before we assess the current state. Then as the employee teams work together to measure and analyze their processes in the next phase, they're able to compare their current performance to the Vision of Perfection they had originally derived.

The activity is easy to facilitate. We just create a set of flipcharts with two sections, and then we ask a representative group of leaders and employees on the transformation team to describe their view of the perfect (1) customer outcomes, process, and technology, and (2) culture of teamwork and performance.

Regardless of what kind of company, department, or business we lead through the discussion, the conversation typically yields uncannily similar results. Amazingly, people who've never heard of Lean end up listing principles that eliminate Lean's classic wastes, as well as the key principles of Engaged Team Performance. We believe that most teams derive the same list because Lean and ETP principles are mostly common sense.

For example, Figure 2 is a Vision of Perfection list that a team made in about 45 minutes, without any prior training in Lean or other business improvement methods.

Identifying your purpose, mission, and definition of perfection can and should produce some angst, as people discuss lofty principles and goals and then compare them to the current state. Don't let that discourage your team; be sure to connect that discussion to finding opportunities for change. Remember, our first step here is to *Commit to Change*; we're supposed to be creating angst at this point. But also understand that people will have strong feelings about the amount of opportunity you find as you begin to look at their organizations and work through a Lean lens.

Client Outcomes, Process, and Technology	Teamwork and Performance

• Quality
  – Zero errors
  – Eliminate shut-offs and late fees (defects)
• High savings impact for clients
• No duplication of roles or work
• Do it right the first time
  – Eliminate errors and rework
  – Quality control / peer review
• One touch & done
• 100% ownership
• End-to-end view of the work
• Scalable capacity to demand
• Automated technology
• Get work done immediately to minimize follow-up
	• Perfect alignment
	  – Everyone understands process, the client, and vertical client industry
	• Consistency among team
	• Common goal as a team
	• Team measures
	  – Visual measures in the workplace
	  – Aligned with goals
	  – Matching accountabilities
	• Strong communication
	• Workforce engagement
	• Collaborative norms
	• Responsible, accountable, and allowed to do the right thing
	• Self-disciplined

Figure 2 Data management team's definition of *perfect*.

Once upon a time, right after the kickoff meeting for a new transformational change effort, we were having a hallway conversation with a leader of the business area that was about to go through the transformation, and the leader started with the words, "I hope we don't find too much opportunity…"

The company had implemented a similar project recently in another department, and that effort had found a substantial (over 40%) opportunity to improve performance and labor efficiency.

Knowing that didn't sound quite right, she stopped herself mid-sentence and started over, "I want to find lots of opportunity, of course. But not *too* much." She stopped again.

"I mean… I want to find as much as we can, just not so much that it embarrasses us…"

"You know what I mean," she said with a wry grin.

We knew what she meant.

THE FROZEN MIDDLE

Hardly anyone likes change. Change is scary. It requires learning new skills and exchanging the comfort of past experience for the risk of a new way of doing things. Even those who embrace change in their personal lives will often still resist it at work.

We often encounter some of that resistance as we lead Lean Engaged Team Performance transformations, of course, and we're sure you see it every day too. But while the perception may be that front-line employees could have the most to lose in organizational change efforts (for example, because they will have to learn new skills or face major changes in their roles), we usually see the worst resistance from the most unlikely of participants: mid-to-senior level leaders. We sometimes call that group the Frozen Middle.

But when you look at the reasons for that resistance, it starts to make sense. Leaders are the most likely to feel a sense of ownership of the existing process, particularly if they have presided over it for a while. They may have designed the existing process and feel that a suggestion for change is an indictment of their past leadership. They worry what others will think. They see themselves as problem-solvers, and it hurts them to find problems that they had perhaps missed seeing in the past.

Regardless, in every change effort there comes a "make or break" moment for each leader where he or she has an opportunity to change or be changed.

A MOMENT OF TRUTH

We had one of those moments with a leader at Ecova as Jana Schmidt's organization began its transformation.

Jennifer Wilson's Utility Expense Management team had just finished a six-week time study, and not an easy one. More than 300 people participated, tracking all of their work every day with to-the-minute precision on each task. Leaders had reviewed the tracking spreadsheets every night, providing feedback to the team members. We were finally ready to look at the data.

Process analysis identified a number of opportunities to consolidate handoffs, prevent non-value-added work, reduce waiting time, and improve quality by reducing data entry errors. The team identified that the diverse functional roles were dispersing accountability and delaying service to clients, while also inhibiting the kind of collaboration that could allow sharing of tasks so that teams could more efficiently overcome daily variation in the various types of incoming work.

Additionally, performance analysis showed that some of the teams were right-staffed, while a few of the larger functions were over-staffed. The total opportunity was more than 10%, which of course was a significant value to a business that size.

We have shown similar numbers to leaders at other companies in the past and have sometimes seen "aversive" behaviors (questioning the data collection methods in ever-greater detail, and then resisting the opportunity to even pilot new ideas). We were pretty sure Wilson would be supportive, but even though we know the leaders pretty well by the time we get to this part of the project, we're never quite sure how they will react when the data hit home.

The moment of truth came. Wilson listened to the data, asked a few questions, and was ready to give us her impression…

"This is so cool!"

When you see an opportunity to change, how will you react?

IT TAKES LEADERSHIP

More than any other tool or concept, a Lean Culture Transformation requires leadership. The senior leader has to commit to change and then share the vision with his or her whole team.

I attended a Lean Six Sigma conference more than ten years ago and had a chance to listen to former General Electric CEO Jack Welch speak and answer questions. During the question session, one person asked Jack, "I'm running a grass-roots Lean Six Sigma effort, trying to get some projects done to show our leadership team the results, and hopefully get them to support a greater investment in continuous improvement over time. Can you please give me some advice on how to best deal with that?"

Jack said, "Find a new job. Next question."

She paused to see if he would say anything more, but then grabbed the microphone again before another person could start a new question, "Seriously, Jack. I'm a mid-level leader in a larger company and I can't get the senior leadership team on board yet. But I don't have the luxury of quitting."

He replied, "Seriously, you need to find a new job. Leaders who don't want to lead change will eventually kill your company. You might as well get out now."

He went on to the next question.

I felt bad for her. My advice would have been to try to do something positive first: try to change your organization for the better by deploying Lean in the area you do control, showing results that will get senior leaders' attention, and seeing if you can get other leaders on board. Sometimes good leaders just need to be shown the value of thinking in a new way, and you probably owe it to them to give them a chance. Then if they see the results and still don't want to change, that's the time to start looking for a new company.

MOVING FORWARD WITH A PURPOSE

As Rich Sheridan explains in *Joy, Inc.*, his purpose can be described in only one word…

> *I now know what I want in business: joy. A pursuit of joy within a business context is not about the pursuit of fame or profit. Humans aspire to a higher purpose. Teams desire to work on goals bigger than themselves. They want to have a lasting and valued effect on the world. They want to make their mark, not for the glory, but for the purpose of bringing delight or ending suffering. Like the Wright brothers, we at Menlo want to fly. We've found that profit, fame, and glory often follow us on this path.*

Every team member at Menlo Innovations can articulate that same purpose.

LEADERSHIP WITH A PURPOSE

In order to move on from here, you have to complete Step 1, *Find Your Purpose: Commit to Change.* We're not saying that it will be easy, but you have to find an inspirational purpose that can light a burning platform for building a Lean Culture and then begin to engage your team in developing, refining, and sharing that purpose across your organization.

Here are some questions to start your journey:

1. Do you really need to change your culture, or can you get better results through executing on existing initiatives?
2. Does your organization have a higher, inspirational purpose that drives you? How can you get all of your team members to understand and buy in to that purpose? How can your team contribute to developing or refining it, so that they can fully buy in?
3. Do you really believe that a Lean Culture of Engaged Team Performance is possible and even desirable?
4. Can you commit to change personally (first!) and organizationally?

We've started this journey by discussing leadership, and we will finish with leadership at the end of the book. Not coincidentally, the key to executing the middle steps is also… leadership.

On we go.

2

Identify Opportunity: Measure and Analyze the Process

In late 2011, a property and casualty insurance company's claims department found that they had opportunities to change core processes, replace their claims computer system, and deploy their branch-office-based team members into a work-from-home environment. The leadership team transformed their department through restructuring and improving processes and performance, leading to a transition of many of the department's employees to work from home. Their story follows the transformational approach we've outlined.

THE NEED FOR CHANGE

Claims adjustment costs at the P&C Insurer were 23% higher than their peer group's; the current organizational structure was inhibiting growth by preventing the company from pricing its products competitively in the market.

THE COMMITMENT

A visionary leader made a commitment to improve processes and performance, which necessitated a restructure of the claims department. The result of the restructure would eliminate physical offices, transform the claims employees into teleworkers, organize a new claims management team, and drive more efficient workflows through the elimination of redundancy.

THE PATH TO IMPROVEMENT

The journey began with data collection. Time studies identified the time it took the claims examiners to adjust different types of claims and determined how many examiners were needed in the reorganized teams. The results of the first time study were astonishing. For every three minutes the teams could save on every claim, the department's labor capacity would increase by one FTE (full time equivalent) person. The time studies also highlighted elements of the claims processes where they could eliminate sources of wasted time. A Lean process streamlining approach reduced handoffs, changed work distribution priorities, and eliminated duplication of work. A supporting "checks and balances" sub-project adjusted approval limits and empowered employees to make decisions within appropriate guidelines.

As the transformation progressed, performance and capacity opportunities grew from the time studies as well. By measuring the amount of work completed and comparing it to the teams' time available, we found that some teams were too busy sometimes while other teams had idle capacity to spare. The result was an opportunity to cross-level work in order to obtain greater efficiency from each team. Some lines of business were able to help others during busy times. The performance opportunities identified were the catalyst for new performance metrics, which were communicated daily to the teams, and the data also drove staffing models that determined the right capacity levels for each team.

THE TRANSITION

The leaders conducted a transition of more than 200 employees from branch sites into their homes, which was not an easy feat. It was clear the new processes and organization would be good but also that accomplishing change would take time and considerable effort. The team knew they had to maintain customer service standards while implementing a seamless transition. Fairness to employees and minimizing impact to quality standards were paramount. Employees were offered the choice of becoming teleworkers or taking a generous retirement/transition package, but very few ended up leaving. Through a well-designed communication strategy, establishment of personal employee ownership and accountability, and a substantial time invested in training, the leaders and teams were able to successfully navigate the transition.

RESULTS

The Lean Engaged Team Performance approach to this organizational redesign effort delivered transformational results for the culture and more than $5 million in annual cost savings (more than half from labor, and the rest from reduction in facility costs), with virtually no negative impact from employee turnover. As normal attrition created open positions, those were left unfilled until they were no longer needed, and existing employees were given opportunities to transition into new roles. The organization continued by pursuing "Lean Ops," a structured and business-focused approach to driving a Lean Culture of Engaged Team Performance (ETP).

These significant Lean improvements couldn't have been accomplished without courageous leadership and engagement at all levels within the organization.

This short story highlights some of the steps that we haven't covered yet. If you look back through the approach the team took, you'll see that the *time study results* were the key to unlocking the opportunities that the leaders thought were there. The time study routinely turns out to be the most enlightening activity in every Lean Culture transformation we lead, helping to build commitment for change as well as providing detailed data on the work, which supports the tactical planning we need in order to design a new organization.

We are going to do a deeper dive now into the concept of time studies here, mostly because they've been under-emphasized in some other transactional Lean applications and we see them as critically important. Experienced Lean practitioners will probably notice that we won't cover other key Lean tools such as Value Stream Maps, Value Added Analysis, and Fishbone Diagrams in the same depth; these process-based analysis methods are integral to Lean, but whole books have been written, for example, on Value Stream Maps, and so we're attempting to focus on important ideas such as time studies that haven't been so well documented in other publications.

DO WE REALLY NEED A TIME STUDY?

Over a decade ago, we got a chance to provide training for a global hotel chain, often in exotic cities such as Paris, Brussels, New Orleans, and Amman. Their global process improvement leader wanted us to augment that training material with a new Lean case study that was specific to their hospitality business, and so we interviewed him about various processes and finally decided to use a housekeeping example.

We asked, "How long does it take a housekeeper to clean a hotel room?"

He quickly replied with a very exact measurement, "32 minutes."

We said, "Wow, that's a specific number. You must have recently done a time study. Where did you run that?" We were surprised, since we had not yet seen many time studies going on in transactional businesses.

"Oh, no," he explained. "We haven't run a time study. But we know that our performance goal for each person is 15 rooms cleaned per day, and so 480 minutes in an 8-hour workday divided by 15 rooms is 32 minutes per room."

It made perfect sense, except for one thing: I stay in a hotel somewhere almost every week, and sometimes I have to leave while the housekeepers clean my room. One thing I know for sure is that it *never* takes that long to clean a hotel room. We eventually crafted a time study that was able to differentiate between check-out and stay-over cleaning, identify some of the other work that housekeepers had to do outside of the rooms (such as replenishing supplies), and set standards that made sense and encouraged teamwork, initiative, and better guest service. We found that a room can really be cleaned in about half of that 32 minutes.

This case study became the perfect example for their leadership team because everyone could relate to the difference in accuracy between a real time study and a back-calculated goal. In addition to getting some great participation in the training, the hotel chain actually changed its housekeeping processes.

THE TIME STUDY

Industrial engineers have been doing time studies on manufacturing processes for decades, so the time study isn't really a new concept. The part that's new is how we engage people in a transactional version of the time study.

The classic industrial engineering time study was designed to study machines. In the mostly transactional businesses of today, the people are the machines. The old method of sending an analyst with a clipboard, pocket protector, and stopwatch to observe the process and time the different steps worked well for the machines, because the machines didn't wonder what the heck was going on.

Nowadays, many Lean Culture transformations are happening in non-manufacturing companies, and so the people there are more cognizant of being watched than machines tend to be. When you send a person to look over employees' shoulders at their computer screens, you can scare and annoy them. And then the Hawthorne effect kicks in (changing subject behavior because they know they're being watched) and results in the analyst collecting non-representative data. That type of time study doesn't work for transactional organizations.

The innovative method we've designed is simply called a "self-reported time study" and works much better. "Self-reported" doesn't mean inaccurate or undisciplined. We create a template for each and every person to collect the data, often in Excel or sometimes in a web-based front-end tied to a larger database, and we ask that each person fill in the worksheet all day every day, usually for a number of weeks, and record a row immediately as they do each task. It sounds like a horribly painful experience to track everyone's work in such a detailed way, but participants later tell us it was enlightening to see where their time actually goes.

Here's how the time study deployment works:

First, we work with employee teams to observe and map processes, ensuring that all tasks and steps that happen in each department or team are on a task list.* That list forms the core of the time study form, which has rows for each activity tracked and columns for the start date, start time, task type, outcome, and stop time of each task. A simple version of the blank template could look like Figure 3.

Name:						
Start Date	Start Time	Task Type	Outcome	Comments	Stop Time	Elapsed

Figure 3 Time study basic template.

Before we proceed, however, we also work with a team of employees to brainstorm the "stratification factors" that might impact task time, for example: product type, location, call type, etc. We'll then decide which factors are important enough to become additional columns that we'll ask employees to capture. If some of those factors are available through existing computer systems, we can just capture an "identification number" from each transaction and look up the associated values later from the system. If not, we have to decide if it's worth it to ask the employees to track those other attributes manually.

Once we add the appropriate columns to the spreadsheet for those additional factors, we create drop-down lists (called "Data Validation" in Excel) to drive consistency and conditional formatting to help the participants identify inappropriate entries (for example, for most businesses, a task that starts at 3:41 AM is probably supposed to be 3:41 PM). The conditional formatting uses IF equations to highlight cells that have unexpected entries so that the individual can check them prior to proceeding. You can see in Figure 4 that the spreadsheet identified a concern with the task that started at 9:32 PM and ended at 9:37 AM, and that's probably one of those AM-PM errors.

---

* We won't cover some of the common Lean tools for that here in great depth, but we'd assure you that Value Stream Maps, Value Added Analysis, Fishbone Diagrams, and other process-based tools are critically important for analyzing processes to find and remove waste, and they are also very useful in preparing for a time study.

Row Number	Employee Name	Start Date	Start Time	Task Type	Outcome	Stop Time	Elapsed	Total Task Time
225	Gina	06/22/15	6:22 AM	59 General admin (reading, general email, PC, etc)	Completed task	6:50 AM	0:28	0:28
226	Gina	06/22/15	6:50 AM	32 New agent programs – administer per program guidelines	Pended to finish task at later time or date	7:38 AM	0:48	0:48
227	Gina	06/22/15	7:38 AM	36 Bonus tracking and reporting	Pended to finish task at later time or date	8:20 AM	0:42	0:37
228	Gina	06/22/15	8:14 AM	32 New agent programs – administer per program guidelines	Completed task	8:19 AM	0:05	0:05
229	Gina	06/22/15	8:21 AM	59 General admin (reading, general email, PC, etc)	Completed task	8:23 AM	0:02	0:02
230	Gina	06/22/15	8:24 AM	44 Unlicensed agent reporting	Completed task	8:25 AM	0:01	0:01
231	Gina	06/22/15	8:39 AM	59 General admin (reading, general email, PC, etc)	Completed task	9:07 AM	0:28	0:28
232	Gina	06/22/15	9:07 AM	32 New agent programs – administer per program guidelines	Pended to finish task at later time or date	9:32 AM	0:25	0:25
233	Gina	06/22/15	9:32 PM	59 General admin (reading, general email, PC, etc)	Completed task	9:37 AM	0:05	0:05
234	Gina	06/22/15	10:00 AM	36 Bonus tracking and reporting	Pended to finish task at later time or date	10:47 AM	0:47	0:47
235	Gine	06/22/15	10:47 AM	32 New agent programs – administer per program guidelines	Pended to finish task at later time or date	11:57 AM	1:10	0:50

Figure 4 Individual time study sheet example.

There are also a couple of interesting entries on the third and fourth lines, where the fourth line is actually an interruption of the task within the third line (the start and stop times of the fourth line are included within the timing of the third line). You'll note that the task time on the third line is five minutes lower than its elapsed time. We train each participant how to use an interruption function that subtracts the interruption from the elapsed time of the task above it.

The interruption concept emphasizes a key point with the time study: we are trying to measure the time for each work task, so we want to make sure we don't collect time for any non-work activities or mix the task times from interrupted tasks. As we introduce the time study format to teams, we tour them through the template together in a conference room using an LCD projector, and we emphasize the need to just collect work time for tasks. We're careful to explain that we know that personal activities such as breaks, lunch, and water-cooler conversations happen at work, and we don't want that time to creep into our measurements. We tell them we don't expect to see eight hours of work in an 8-hour day and we don't care how much time they report, as long as the task times are true.

So in the example above, you'll notice some gaps between the end time of a task and the start time of the next task, and that's just fine. We'll assume that was a personal break or other non-work activity, and we won't worry about that time. To reinforce that concept with participants, I usually tell a short story about another time study launch...

We had just started a time study the day before, and I was helping the transformation project team do the typical "overnight checking" that we use to provide feedback every morning to each participant for the first few days. We find that it's really important to provide feedback to everyone at the beginning, because almost everyone makes a few mistakes initially. Most people start turning in perfect spreadsheets on day two or three.

One person in a "work from home" role turned in his first spreadsheet that first night, and I saw that he had a 50-minute entry with a task type of "Other" and a comment out to the right that said "Shower." Ugh! We really don't want to know how long that kind of stuff takes.

Here are some of the instructions that we typically give:

1. Please record every work activity that you do during the day *on a separate row*. We are *not* recording non-work activities such as lunch time or breaks on separate lines, although those may count as interruptions. Just record work tasks. We are not recording any personal time, and we know that every work day has some of that in it. We are just interested in measuring the work.

2. When you start working on a task, immediately go to the tracking spreadsheet and enter the basic information (task type, start time, and so on). It's particularly important to record the start time up front, since that would be difficult to estimate after you're done with the task. Please record the time to the nearest minute.

3. If you're interrupted during the task, there's a place to record the type of interruption (an incoming phone call, for example) and the time it took. That time will be subtracted from the overall work time so that we can accurately calculate the time it takes to do each kind of task. You should only record interruptions that happened in the *middle* of doing a task, not things you did in between tasks (before starting the next task). If the interruption is itself a work task, record it on the next line; if it is a personal discussion or event, you don't need to record a new line for it.

4. If some of the blanks in a row turn pink, that "conditional formatting" is an indication that the spreadsheet expects data to be entered there. If you enter something and the cell remains pink, it's an indicator that the spreadsheet expected something different, perhaps in a different format. For example, the sheet expects times to be entered in the following format: 12:30 PM (there's a space needed between the time and the AM or PM). Also, if you enter a time that doesn't make sense (3:30 AM), the cell may stay pink to indicate that the response wasn't what the sheet expected.

5. Many of the columns include answer options in drop-down lists, but if the task or category you need isn't there, please select "Other" and then explain with some detail in the comments section out to the right. Please make sure you're selecting the best task description, and if you find that you're selecting "Other" frequently, tell us immediately because we'll want to add a new task type for that activity.

6. All of the drop-downs and conditional formatting (pink highlights) will work on all of the rows, unless you copy-paste or insert/delete cells or rows. That will mess up the formatting. If your conditional formatting gets broken, tell us and we'll help get your data back into the right format.

7. Use the same spreadsheet for the entire time, and continue to add to the bottom of it as you go. We recommend you save it often. By the end, you may have a copy saved for each day, each one with the newest date; the newest will have all the data since the beginning of the collection.

As we discussed above, we check each participant's spreadsheet nightly for the first few days, looking for errors but also for inaccurate entries that may indicate integrity issues. These we rarely find. The vast majority of people attempt to do a diligent job of tracking their time.

Martin Sieh, who leads Ecova's Sales and Operations, explains:

> The time study is one of the most critical portions of the process. What is most important is that the teams involved in the study need to know it is not a witch hunt. The goal is to understand each task they complete and how long it takes. We want to find out all the things they do and what we can do to change and improve.
>
> To do this the teams must hear from leadership that no negative actions will take place. Leaders need to hear and see the hard truth. Then we will change things to improve the work they complete.
>
> To achieve the desired goals, the information the employees report must be reviewed daily to ensure it makes sense. If employees do not complete it correctly, provide immediate feedback so the data are appropriate. Only through daily review and immediate feedback will appropriate data be collected.
>
> Then once the data are collected, analysis can be completed and decisions made about how to change, driving the improvement.
>
> An additional question that must be contested at the leadership level is, "Why not just jump to the time study immediately; why complete all this other process mapping work?" Doing that process mapping together helps us decide what elements need to be collected in the time study, but the most important rationale is that the teams need to build trust and buy into the change process by being involved along the way.

Strong execution of a detailed time study both creates foundational data to enable change and engages the entire team in the process. When we later use the data to identify opportunities and set standards, the entire team can feel comfortable that the information came from a representative and accurate source that they're confident in trusting: themselves!

TIME STUDY RESULTS

The time study always yields some amazing results. We'll share some typical examples in the sections below.

Proportions of Time Spent by Task Type

Most importantly, the time study allows us to quantify the amount of time spent on every activity in the business, which will then inform the cost-benefit analysis of proposed process and organizational changes. While the data don't really change the Lean principles that we use to identify change opportunities, they do help quantify the value of those concepts, and sometimes the data can be very useful in helping to remove doubts about that value.

For example, one of Ecova's client service teams found some interesting results in their data after their 4-week time study. For this team of 10 employees, the top 12 task types (out of more than 60 tasks) accounted for over 73% of the work. Those top 12 task types are shown in Figure 5, sorted by total time spent during the time study and recalculated as both a percentage of time and a proportion of the 10-person team (in FTE).

Until you read each of the task types on the list and consider what they mean, the opportunity identified by these numbers may not pop out at you. But when you consider that this particular client service team's purpose was to communicate with the company's clients, you will quickly see that general admin, internal coordination, internal follow-ups, system downtime, internal state of the client calls, and other meetings and activities toward the bottom of the list all have one thing in common: *they're not client-facing work!* Since those tasks don't transform the product in a way that the client would want (and be willing to pay for), they aren't considered value-added tasks.

The three highlighted cells in Figure 5 (client touchpoint calls, platform upgrades and support, and coordinating client requests) totaled less than 14% of the team's time and were the only value-added work on the Top 12 list. In total, the non-value-added work was more than four times the amount of value-added work, which is quite typical for real processes but nonetheless a bit surprising for the leaders and teams when they saw it calculated that way.

The results of the time study were quite eye-opening for the team, but we had to be very careful to make sure everyone interpreted the causes and potential solutions the right way.

Task Types		Total	Percent	FTE
21	General admin (reading, general email, PC, etc.)	312:50:00	22.5%	2.25
9	Internal coordination of services / delivery (proactive, not an "issue")	120:19:00	8.7%	0.87
5	Follow-up with internal people to ask for updates or actions (ongoing)	117:25:00	8.5%	0.85
10	Client touchpoint calls	98:08:00	7.1%	0.71
27	System downtime	59:16:00	4.3%	0.43
8	Internal state of the client calls	53:54:00	3.9%	0.39
15	Platform upgrades and support	45:51:00	3.3%	0.33
3	Coordinate client request (first report from client)	43:33:00	3.1%	0.31
23	Updating SmartSheet	43:31:00	3.1%	0.31
11	Business Reviews (e.g., QBR prep and attendance)	43:00:00	3.1%	0.31
25	Meeting	40:21:00	2.9%	0.29
20	Managing tasks in Salesforce	39:48:00	2.9%	0.29

Figure 5 Client management task time.

The numbers were not showing a behavior problem; this performance wasn't anyone's fault! The amount of time spent internally coordinating was just a result of the organizational design. That client service role was the "middle man and woman" in between a large number of other internal roles that served different client needs. The team had already identified the fact that a number of internal people were involved in every client situation and/or meeting, and the company even had a catch-phrase for that: the "Eight-Legged Monster" was the group of four internal people who had to collaborate on every issue and show up to every call and meeting. The data just helped us quantify the cost of that current organizational design.

While the team had already discussed the idea of combining some of the operational and client management roles, the data really gave some credibility to that somewhat scary organizational change concept. We'll discuss some of the organizational changes that Ecova made in a later chapter.

Standard Time Per Task

Another useful analysis concept turns out to be the "standard time" for each task. By adding up the time spent by task type and then dividing by the number of completions, we are able to estimate the average amount of time that each task takes, as well as study the variation (e.g., standard deviation) by task type. Figure 6 is an example from a life insurance operation.

In Figure 6, just a subset of a longer list of tasks from a workflow system in a life insurance business, we can see that not all tasks require an equal effort. For example, the higher-volume task of an Agent Pay Adjustment (AGNTADJ) takes a little under 5.5 minutes to complete each iteration, while the lower-volume task of 1035 Exchange (1035EXCH) requires almost 18.5 minutes per completion. For those of you who've worked in a life insurance business, you won't find that time difference too surprising, but you also might be beginning to feel the value of such a precise measurement. We will explain in later chapters how to use this data for setting standards, measuring efficiencies, designing staffing models, and communicating with visual data.

Task Types	Total Time	Count of Quantity	Time per Completion
1035EXCH	4:55:00	16	0:18:26
ADDTLMONEY	9:51:00	73	0:08:06
AGNTADJ	32:05:00	361	0:05:20
AGNTADJE	9:02:00	94	0:05:46
BACKSCAN	0:10:00	3	0:03:20
CANCEL	2:24:00	17	0:08:28
CHECKRQST	5:32:00	47	0:07:04

Figure 6 Standard time for tasks.

This analysis takes an important Lean concept, *standard work*, to a new level. In addition to documenting what the work is and making it repeatable, we learn how long each work type should take. There are also more complex methods for analyzing work that has higher variation; see the book *Building Engaged Team Performance* for a detailed case study analysis using multiple regression to quantify the multi-variable drivers of variation in task time.

Performance Efficiency

Finally, another very interesting view of the data is the "performance summary" that shows how much work time each team reported each day. As you may suspect, though, we're much more interested in the organizational implications of the results and not at all interested in individual performance. We don't want to use this self-reported data for performance management. In a later chapter, we'll use the standard time data described in the section above to design a new team performance management approach, relying almost solely on team performance feedback rather than individual accountability. All that said, the amount of time reported by team in the time study can be a great indicator of relative efficiency levels that we need to investigate further.

When we launch the time study, we're careful to set the agreement with everyone, particularly leaders, that nobody will be rewarded or punished for any of the data they report, as long as it's true. We want to encourage accurate reporting of the time study data, and so we are careful not to establish a goal for how much work time will be reported. As we discussed in an earlier example, we just tell everyone that we certainly don't expect to see eight hours of work in an 8-hour day, and we explain that we'll be using the data for quantifying opportunities as well as setting standards. We don't want them to try to work any faster or slower than usual, and we need them to follow the standard process and do quality work while we're measuring the time.

We commit that nobody will be rewarded or punished for telling the truth, and then we're very interested to see what the truth tells us.

When we add up the time that each person spent working and then divide by the number of days worked (adjusting for any vacation or partial days worked as well), we are able to calculate a number of hours per day tracked. Our typical method for that calculation is to remove the general administrative* category from the time and then compare the team averages to a typical "busy team" that would have between 6.5 and 7 hours of work done in an 8-hour day worked.

Here's how that math typically works:

- Time present on-site: 8.5 hours (with an unpaid 30-minute lunch period)
- Paid work time in a day: 8 hours
- Less general overhead: 1 – 1.5 hours
  - Breaks and other free time: 0.5 – 0.75 hours
  - General administrative time: 0.5 – 0.75 hours
- Expected work time available: 6.5 – 7 hours

General Admin time usually includes startup and shutdown of computers, clearing of general internal emails a few times per day, reading general communications, and other non-specific work.

Figure 7 is a real example from the Lean Culture transformation at Ecova, some of the data that Jennifer Wilson thought was so cool in the previous chapter. Obviously, some teams were much busier than others.

Row Labels	Sum of Time	Sum of Days Worked	Work/Day	Current FTE	Hours Scheduled	FTE	Gain
Account Specialist I	3973:49:50	689	5:46:04	42	8	38.2	3.8
Account Specialist II	3482:12:00	588	5:55:14	34	8	31.5	2.5
Billing Support	4828:39:07	883	5:28:08	57	8	49.7	7.3
Client Service Representative	2420:25:00	441	5:29:19	28	8	24.5	3.5
Data Information Specialist	10025:33:00	1503	6:40:21	91	8	93.0	-2.0
EDI Support	481:33:00	68	7:04:54	5	8	5.4	-0.4
Invoice Analyst I	5465:14:00	1019	5:21:50	61	8	52.3	8.7
Mailroom Specialist	1423:21:00	195	7:18:27	12	8	13.2	-1.2
Template Specialist	1209:49:00	203	5:57:22	12	8	11.2	0.8
Grand Total	33310:35:57	5588	5:57:39	342	8	318.9	23.1

Figure 7 Performance efficiency by team.

As with other data about time spent on different types of tasks, we have to make sure that everyone views this information in a positive way. When we see a difference in time per day reported by a team, we don't presume that one team is hard-working and another team is lazy. First, we look at their work backlogs to make sure everyone is keeping up with their workflow. (As is usually the case, they all were.) And once we verify that, we know that the differences are caused by workload, not behaviors. Lower workload isn't the team's fault.

We know that teams with lower workloads can't be efficient because there isn't any more work to do, and so we make sure that leaders understand that the lower numbers aren't caused by lazy team members; they're caused by poor workflow and organization design. And that's a leadership opportunity that we'll tackle in a later phase of the transformation, when we *Transform: Organize the Team*.

The overall opportunity in Jennifer's department at Ecova (if each team were working 6.5 hours in an 8-hour day) was 23 FTE, or about $1 million per year in potential labor efficiency. For a growing company with normal attrition and turnover, balancing the team sizes with the workload would generate a huge potential gain that wouldn't require any adverse impacts on the team members. Right-sizing the teams for the work would just result in fewer people to hire and train when attrition or growth occurred.

And so that's what they did. We'll tell the rest of that Ecova reorganization story in later chapters.

BACK TO QUALITY

In addition to work time and efficiency, the other key measures that illuminate the opportunities for a business, of course, are product and service quality. Some of that information can come from the time study too (for example, calculating the proportion of incoming work items that are arriving "in good order" instead of missing information). But most organizations often have other measures in place for monitoring quality, so we'll discuss the general concepts of designing those as well.

Like many of you, we started leading teams during the 1980s and 1990s. During that time, great concepts from the past 60 years were packaged into a single word that described a vision of everything we should be... Quality.

Quality meant doing the right thing for the customer, delivering the right thing to the customer at the right time, and reducing cost by doing it right the first time. Those of us who worked in manufacturing plants grew up surrounded by control charts and other components of statistical process control. We learned to discern the difference between common variation and special causes, and we learned to manage with data. We listened to experts such as W. Edwards Deming, who said that great

Quality was an outcome of leadership, process, and human performance. And then we moved on to cooler-sounding concepts such as Lean Six Sigma, which have taken Quality concepts to another level in driving efficiency and effectiveness.

Unfortunately, a couple of decades later, we now may have started taking Quality for granted, so we sometimes have to be reminded to go… Back to Quality.

QUALITY TODAY

Poor quality today can still drive vast hidden costs, just as it did decades ago. And with the proliferation of non-manufacturing businesses, improving transactional quality has become a huge opportunity.

Some transactional businesses we know use statistical sampling to measure quality. Some just use 100% peer checking. Some focus their quality controls on monitoring processes; some focus only on driving human performance. Some collect more data than others.

Sadly, many quality assurance (QA) programs today don't follow yesterday's quality control (QC) principles. For example, we've seen some peer checking processes that inspect 100% of outputs, yielding decent quality at a huge cost (one team we measured recently had 28% of work time spent on checking). Because they may want the same favor in return someday, peers often prefer to find and fix defects without even recording that the defect existed, so those organizations often miss the opportunity to use data upstream to improve the process. As the saying goes, "You can't inspect Quality into a process," and actually we find that the perceived safety net of a 100% quality checker can cause the person upstream doing the work to feel less accountable, making quality worse instead of better.

Rather than trying to find and fix every defect, quality checking is best when used as a way to control the process and drive accountability for performance, thereby *preventing* future defects. The best way to do that is to randomly sample a small proportion of tasks completed, so that you can track and trend defects, isolate and mistake-proof their causes, and provide appropriate feedback to individuals and teams. But even some organizations that sample their work for quality control appropriately can still miss opportunities to get the most out of their data.

During one company's Lean transformation, we led a project to measure the quality of their data entry process, and at first blush everything looked great—they were sampling the process appropriately to drive accountability, and their team members had an average score of 99.3% on their quality checks on a "line item score" level. Though not yet at a Six Sigma level of performance, that's quite high for a human data entry process. And then we measured the quality from the "unit-level" perspective of the customer, and the quality was only 88.3%. It seems that there are multiple line items in each delivery to the customer, and so the "line item score" didn't really represent the customer-felt results... who knew?

Interestingly, leaders knew both numbers, but they were only using the 99.3% number in performance accountability discussions with the team members.

"The 88.3% number makes people feel bad," one leader explained.

The team's performance had been hovering in that range for quite a while, and everyone had gotten accustomed to seeing those numbers. And besides, other roles later in the process caught and fixed most of those defects before they reached the end customers, so there really wasn't much harm, right?

It turns out that rework was costing them quite a bit more than they thought. After an employee survey across the organization to estimate the amount of rework that data entry issues caused, we calculated the potential cost of poor quality at 200 full-time equivalent (FTE) people. Interestingly, that was twice the number of people who worked in the data entry team.

As the leaders started sharing the real results with their teams, they challenged everyone to look for process improvement and mistake-proofing opportunities and stay focused on quality from a performance perspective. They shifted the balance of team metrics, which had been focused almost solely on production volumes, so that quality and productivity were both highlighted. To enable those measures to have more impact, they asked the Quality Control department to keep up with quality checks in "real time" (daily) and report team results much more frequently (daily and weekly instead of monthly). And they started sharing individuals' quality stories and training opportunities at every daily team huddle.

Over three months, they cut their defect rates in half, and they have since sustained the new level of quality through today.

QUALITY PRINCIPLES FOR THE FUTURE

So as we go "back to the future" of Quality, here are a few principles to consider:

1. Use appropriate statistical sampling calculations* to decide how much data to collect, how to stratify that data, and how to randomize the collection process. Get help from one of those Six Sigma Black Belt trained people at your company who know how to do that kind of analysis.

A good source for statistical sampling calculations is The Six Sigma Way Team Fieldbook, *or you can use Minitab software, which has great help and tutorial functions.*

2. Train a separate team of quality inspectors, instead of having peers check each other.
3. Measure quality from the *customer's* perspective. Understand the defects that are getting to customers, both in quantity and criticality, and work to improve them.
4. Measure quality from a *process* perspective. Look for trends and root causes, so that *you* can focus improvement efforts on prevention and mistake-proofing. Understand the cost of poor quality, including inspection, rework, client management, and other activities your teams do to mitigate problems.
5. Measure quality trends from a *team* perspective. Show the team the tough numbers so they can challenge themselves to perform better. Don't sugar-coat it.
6. And yes, hold *individuals* accountable for quality as well, but start with the presumption that all individuals are doing their best, and look for process root causes and technology solutions to mistake-proof the human work.

Your quality-checking regimen should be tuned to accomplish all of those goals, and that may require you to calculate the sampling numbers and share the results a few different ways.

All of this drives to an important conclusion: *good quality is always cheaper than poor quality!*

LEADING AS YOU MEASURE AND ANALYZE THE PROCESS

As you have seen, Step 2 in a Lean Culture transformation is to *Identify Opportunity: Measure and Analyze the Process*. We discussed the value of running self-reported time studies and gathering data on quality measures, and we learned how to execute both of those measurement approaches.

We also briefly discussed some other key Lean tools, particularly Value Stream Maps, that should be used for mapping and visualizing the impact of waste in processes. We recommend the book *Learning to See* from the Lean Enterprise Institute for more on that critical tool.

Producing these measurements sounds like a lot of work, and it is. But measuring work time and quality will deliver critical information that the organization will use in later phases to streamline processes, fix problems, right-staff teams, and design performance controls. These measures are the key to unlocking opportunities.

The leadership challenge in measuring and analyzing the process mostly results from the time and effort that it takes to do that measurement well. As we've said, a time study is hard work to plan and execute, and it requires diligent effort from all of the team members who are gathering their own data for a few weeks. Leaders have to confidently articulate the reasons for the time study, and some of the best results have come from teams where the leaders participated in the time study as well. Everyone learns something important about where and how they are spending their time.

Here are some questions to prepare leaders for the measurement effort:

1. Do you already track quality data and use it to improve performance? Do you measure client experience and satisfaction as well? Are there opportunities to measure quality better?

2. Do you already know how long it takes to do each task in your operation? If not, who is going to do all the work of designing time study tracking sheets and collecting data? Some organizations already have dedicated resources who are trained in Lean Six Sigma data collection, but even many of those people haven't done this kind of time study before. And your IT team may have access to some data from existing systems, but that data may not have accurate task times. So you have to decide who's going to lead this effort, then make sure those people develop the appropriate skills.

3. How will you ensure that your whole team understands your positive intent for gathering this information? If people start to believe that the purpose is to cut jobs or punish lazy employees, you won't get accurate data. Design a communication plan.

4. Who will analyze the data, and how will you communicate the results to leaders and team members?

5. Will you and your leadership team set the example by participating as well?

6. What do you think you will find when you collect work time for every task from every person? Do you already see the opportunities in your organization?

We hope you get to experience the pain and power of collecting the time study data. We'll refer to the time study results over and over as we proceed.

Now we'll talk more about some of the different types of opportunities we're hoping to root out.

3
Drive Value: Streamline the Process

Everything you do is a process, and we find that Lean provides a new lens to help you see every process in a different way. Ultimately, every process must drive the maximum value for customers with the minimum effort. Sounds simple, right?

EZB

In 2009, the CEO of a bank affiliated with a Fortune 500 company articulated a vision for making the company a place where customers found it "easy to do business." Within the company this became known as EZB. He wanted to improve both process and performance in his team, and he did a great job of continually repeating that vision: the purpose was to improve the customer experience, not just save money.

They started a Lean Culture transformation.

As we worked together on the transformation, we did all of the previously mentioned steps, building a commitment for change, creating detailed value stream maps to analyze the entire business process infrastructure, and measuring their processes with a time study.

One of their core processes was the final payment out to the customer when an account was closed remotely, and this of course was the last step in the life-cycle of a customer.

When we asked some bank team members what the customer requirements were for the process, we got some interesting answers:

- The customers just wanted their money as soon as they could get it, of course
- The regulators and internal risk controls required that they receive a signed request form and verify the identity of the customer before paying them and closing the account
- The internal standard for turn-around time to cut a check was 8 business days after receiving the form in the mail or by fax

The 8-day turnaround time seemed a bit out of place, since the customers wanted their money as soon as possible, but a team member was quick to explain: "Well, since this is their last transaction and they're leaving us, we prioritize other work ahead of this type." It didn't really seem "EZB," but the explanation made sense. Until we looked deeper.

Lean process streamlining theories look for many types of waste, and as a reminder from a previous chapter, here is the classic list of eight wastes:

1. Transportation – Moving people, products, or information from one location to another
2. Inventory – Storing products or documentation; backlog of work in process
3. Motion – Movement within a work cell; movement of a mouse inside a computer
4. Waiting – Waiting for parts, information, instructions, tools, tasks, or work to arrive
5. Over-production – Making more than is required by the customer
6. Over-processing – Doing more work or effort than the customer requires
7. Defects – Errors, rework, scrap, or incorrect documentation
8. Skills – Under-utilized human capabilities

When we mapped the current-state process for those account closure distributions, we saw a lot of motion, transportation, waiting, and over-processing (see Figure 8), but the wastes weren't quite so obvious until we talked to bank employees about the process.

There was obviously some transportation (to and from the downtown imaging operation), so we started simply by asking why. There's always a good reason, of course.

Q: Why do we transport the payment forms downtown for imaging?

A: We have a high-speed image system and a dedicated team down there, and they can do the imaging same-day and return the forms to us within 24 hours.

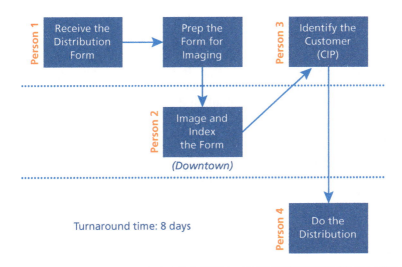

Figure 8 Account closure payment current-state process.

> **Q:** Why do we have to receive the form at our facility and prep it before sending it for imaging?
>
> **A:** The imaging team doesn't know our work well enough to identify the form and capture the indexing (identifying) information, so we open the mail, separate those forms, look up and write the indexing information on them, and then put a barcoded coversheet on each one so that they'll scan properly. We do that on the day the forms arrive in the mail, then send them downtown that night to be scanned the next morning. The forms come back that afternoon.
>
> **Q:** So after we get the forms back from downtown, do we work from the forms or the image?
>
> **A:** Our operations team doesn't have access to the image. We just work from the forms.
>
> **Q:** Why do we image it ahead of time, then?
>
> **A:** Oh, there's a different reason for that. The call center needs the image. In the past, we used to just work from the forms, but we found that the call center couldn't answer questions when the customer called to make sure we got their form and find out where it was in the process. So now when they call, the call center can instantly look up their form and see when it arrived.

> Q: What does the contact center tell the customer?
>
> A: They just remind the customer that the check will be sent out within 8 business days of the arrival date. The customers usually know that, but sometimes they need the money sooner and try to expedite it. Sometimes the check is already in the mail, and sometimes we haven't done the payment processing yet.
>
> Q: Okay, so what do we do when we get the forms back from imaging?
>
> A: Our Customer Identification Process (CIP) person validates the identity of the requestor, and then we place the form in a folder that corresponds to its due date, which is 8 business days from when it arrived.
>
> Q: And then the form waits there until that date?
>
> A: Right, we pull the folder each morning for that due date and process the payments in it.

Interestingly, process wastes that are pretty obvious to a neutral observer aren't quite so obvious to people who have been working within a process as it evolved. The time study helped to quantify and demonstrate the opportunities more clearly:

- The whole process, including all of the steps shown that occurred within the bank (but not at the imaging center) took only *5.5 minutes* per form, with an 8-day turnaround time.
- Most of the 8 days was spent waiting, of course. It takes 5.5 minutes to do the work, whether it happens on Day 1 or Day 8.
- When a customer called the contact center for a status update, it took *5 minutes* of the contact center's time to verify their identity and answer the question.
- The "image prep" step took 40 seconds if done before the payment, but it could be accomplished in *zero seconds* during the account closure work (while waiting for the computer screens to update) to allow post-task imaging for record-keeping if we hadn't needed the image ahead of time for the call center.

Depending on how we identified the problem and which wastes we wanted to reduce, we might have proposed some sub-optimal solutions. For example, keeping the 8-day standard and working from the image instead of the paper might have saved a little bit of time and seemed more "paperless," but still would have resulted in fielding additional calls from the customers who wanted their money.

We decided to challenge the paradigms of paperless work and waiting to do it. What if we just did both the customer identification and the payment right when the form arrived? Then we wouldn't need to image it until afterward. The new process looked a lot simpler (see Figure 9).

It sounded logical, but there was a key objection: "What if we get behind? Sometimes we get a lot of closure requests all on one day. If we don't get them all done, the call center won't be able to find the form when the customer calls."

Here was the somewhat unexpected answer: "You can't get behind. We have to design the process to get everything done every day, and we have to cross-train people in different roles to create capacity to handle the natural variation in workload."

While "don't get behind" was easy to say, we all knew that it would be hard to do. In fact, it took six more months of work to cross-train the team and create a plan for handling the busy season for account closures, which happened in the first three months of every year. We used volume data to model the workload and arranged to have the right capacity available to meet the demand every day.

But we're getting ahead of ourselves here in the story, because we didn't have to figure out yet how to make a whole reorganization work; we just had to prove the value of the consolidated process in getting the work done in one day. So the team agreed to try out the new process.

A week later, we had piloted a one-step start-to-finish process, cleared out the entire backlog of waiting payments in the pending folders, and then turned off the pre-task imaging process and switched to post-task imaging. Cutting out the pre-task imaging saved 40 seconds, and we gained another 20 seconds from consolidating the handoff from the CIP person to the payment person. In the prior process, the CIP person and the payment person would each do batches of 5-10 documents in those separate tasks, rather than doing a single payment from start to finish. There's always a small duplication of effort when a person has to read a document as they pick up work after a handoff, and so going to a one-touch process saved that time. This was an example of single-piece flow, a key Lean concept.

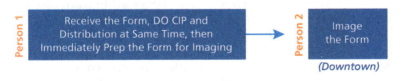

Figure 9 Future-state account closure payment process.

We saw an 18 percent reduction in labor for that task (4.5 minutes per payment instead of 5.5 minutes), which generated capacity that we were able to shift to other backlog-reduction efforts in processes such as returned mail. And we noticed some collateral benefits too:

- Calls related to closure payments into the contact center fell by 30 percent; we were getting the work done so fast that customers didn't have to call any more to ask where it was.
- Processing errors decreased. We realized that having the same person do the customer identification and immediately proceed to issuing the payment *one at a time instead of batching the separate tasks* resulted in fewer chances to key in a dollar amount or an account number improperly.

The transformation was a huge win, both for customers and for the team. The pilot helped team members intuitively understand the value of serving customers quickly, and the transformation freed the employees to do the right things for customers. Faster and better was cheaper too!

THE SPIRIT OF LEAN

Lean and Engaged Team Performance (ETP) theories say that "single-piece flow with as few handoffs as possible" is the most efficient way to run a process. Henry Ford's assembly line revolutionized the world of manufacturing by allowing specialization of skills; sadly, right after that almost everyone started over-specializing almost everything. The classic production line can create defects, excess work-in-process inventory, over-production, non-value-added work within handoffs, over-checking, under-used human capital, and so on. Somewhat counter-intuitively, all of the wastes in the "eight wastes" list can come from an over-specialized assembly line.

For leaders, the hardest part of challenging the existing process may be that some of those same leaders helped to create or evolve the current state process. As we saw in the story above, the handoffs, motion, and other non-value-added work were probably created with the best of intentions. Nevertheless, when team members start to learn about Lean process streamlining and the eight wastes, they will soon start to see opportunities, but they may worry about the consequences of calling out the poor decisions of the past.

Senior leaders need to create a safe place for these conversations. You have to shift from a Culture of Blame to a Culture of Learning by telling everyone, especially junior leaders, "I don't blame you for any decisions you made before you learned about these Lean principles, but I'll hold you accountable for learning to apply the principles better in the future."

As we've shown in the EZB story above, the most substantial waste opportunity is usually in handoffs, so we'll spend a little more time discussing those with another story below. While you certainly want to streamline the value-added work as much as possible, you should always observe the ultimate impact and unintended consequences of the roles, handoffs, and process steps you create; when you do, you'll sometimes find that having one resource do the job start-to-finish (with appropriate technology and support, and perhaps a few rational handoffs when some work really requires special skills) has a lower total cost than some of the alternatives.

Here's another example.

It's a Crappy Job...

A few winters ago, my daughter Aspen went to interview for a job, and I drove her over to the pet resort (a fancy name for kennel) where she wanted to work.

The pet resort had a really interesting concept called a "working interview" – basically that means that they get a free day of work from a teenager before deciding if the position is a fit for both parties. Some companies pay for that, but this one didn't. It seemed like a scam to me.

I was sure about that once I heard what time we had to be there: 6:00 am on a Saturday morning! But I dropped her off and made sure she got safely inside, went home to go back to sleep, and finally got the call four hours later that she was done.

When I picked her up and asked how the interview went, she shrugged and said it was okay. She liked the animals; she didn't like cleaning their cages quite so much. And she said she got to walk the dogs outside...

Uh-oh. I was worried – it's dark until about 7:00 am in the winter, and I didn't want her to be somewhere unsafe by herself. I asked where she was walking them.

But she said it was fine, "There's a large, lighted field with a fence, and I just walk the dogs around in there."

I'm not sure why I asked, "Do you have to pick up the dog poop?"

"No," she said matter-of-factly, "I just flag it."

But Someone Has To Do It!

I asked, "Who picks up the poop, then?" I was wondering who would be paid even less than the entry-level teenager sitting in front of me. And I have to admit, I immediately started to imagine that she might say...

> *Well, first an "imaging" person comes and takes a photo of it with their iPhone, and then we have an "indexer" identify the type, size, location, and consistency of it. We then send the image "offshore" for processing to record that information in the workflow system...*

OK, not really.

But her answer was even more predictable, in a business-realistic sort of way: "I don't know; it must be somebody else. It's not my job."

CRAPPY HANDOFFS

Businesses design processes with handoffs for the best of intentions:

- As referenced in the "offshoring" example above, sometimes the handoff pays for itself, when a specialist (either on-shore or off-shore) can learn a specific role better or accomplish it more cost-effectively.
- Sometimes a certain task is just too hard for too many people to learn or requires special tools or licensing.
- Or it needs to be done at a different time, for example, so the dog-walker isn't distracted by having to stop too often to pick up after the dogs.

We're not saying that those reasons aren't important, but we often find that businesses also fail to take a number of unintended consequences into account:

- *Additional work:* the handoff always creates some additional work to transfer the task. In the pet resort's case, planting the flag is an extra step that wouldn't be needed if she were just picking up along the way. In other businesses, a workflow system may mask the additional work by making it seem easy to move items around, but if you look deeper you'll see "handoff forms" and other documentation requirements to enter and transfer pertinent information, and all of those take some extra time. We've seen some hand-off forms that took longer to fill out than the task they were handing off.
- *Missed handoffs:* what if she fails to flag one of the "left behind" items? Someone else could encounter it by accident! In other organizations, the handoff may create a need to occasionally go back to the originator to clarify the instructions, rescan an image, or gather more information, and it sometimes can also lead to higher defect rates.
- *Accountability:* handoffs can disperse accountability too, by allowing various roles to blame each other for missed handoffs or errors in translation.
- *Aging:* what if it rains or snows in between the flagging and the pickup? It's not going to get any easier to pick up, and it might get harder (or, in this case, softer). In other businesses, handoffs cause a need for tracking of the work's location and sometimes make the work more difficult when the time comes to do it.

- *Backlog:* no pun intended (okay, maybe pun intended). More steps result in more waiting time in between steps, which in turn allows more aging and drives customer questions, status calls, and service issues. We've seen some cases where the time to track the work backlog and answer customer questions about it was more than doing the task itself, similar to our story earlier about the account closure payments.

An old friend once said, "Handoffs always cost you more than you think they will and save you less than you think they will." (Thanks, Amy Friedrich!)

Every handoff is there for a reason, of course. We're just asking you to challenge the reasons. I never found out why the pet resort used the poop flags, though, because my daughter decided to look for a different career path.

5S: WORKPLACE ORGANIZATION

The two stories above got us thinking about the Spirit of Lean, and the whole point is that leaders need to get everybody looking for those eight wastes, challenging non-value-added processes and handoffs, and sustaining improved performance. The Lean process streamlining tool that engages people the best is called 5S. The 5S acronym stands for five Japanese words, *seiri, seiton, seiso, seiketsu,* and *shitsuke*. Translated into English, they all still start with an S:

- **Sort** (Seiri) – Remove unnecessary items and dispose of them properly. Make work easier by eliminating obstacles and non-value added steps. Identify the eight wastes in the process and remove them.

- **Set in Order** (Seiton) – Also starting to be called "Streamline," identify a home (the best location) for all remaining items: a place for everything and everything in its place. Set work-in-process limits. Put process steps and work stations in the optimum order.

- **Shine** (Seiso) – Clean everything, inside and out. Clean work areas not only drive efficiency, but more importantly they incite pride in the team members.

- **Standardize** (Seiketsu) – Agree upon the rules for maintaining and controlling the first 3S steps in a repeatable way. Use visual controls to highlight compliance.

- **Sustain** (Shitsuke) – Ensure cultural buy-in to the 5S standards through communication, measures, training, self-discipline, and leadership.

Many organizations combine the concept of "5S" (employee engagement in organizing the workplace) with "Kaizen" (employee teams focused on incremental improvement), which usually includes training employee-led teams to execute a blend of both types of improvements on the work floor. By exposing whole teams to Lean principles and then giving them time and accountability to lead changes, the leadership team can empower everyone to improve their own work. People are more likely to support changes that they and their peers helped to design.

One of my first process improvement roles was in leading a Kaizen program at Coors Brewing Company almost 20 years ago. In our first year, we started with goals related to saving money, and we got the program off to a good start. Facilitating a different Kaizen effort every other week was just a fantastic experience for me. I thought we were doing great.

We did an employee survey at the end of the year, though, and we found a stunning correlation: people who had already participated in one of our Kaizen events were overwhelmingly supportive of the effort, but people who had not participated were quite suspicious of management's motives for the program and were very negative about their opinions of its value.

The next year we set a new goal: we would succeed only if 80% of the individuals in our over-1000-person division had been recognized for participating on a Kaizen team that accomplished some kind of positive change by the end of that year. We found that we had a lot of facilitation work that we needed to accomplish. Our goal went from financial to cultural, and it incidentally drove even greater financial results the next year.

Toyota drives engagement through Kaizen. Their organization uses an "A3" form (so-called because the Toyota version was designed on large A3 paper) as a single-sheet record of the results of a Kaizen effort. Tellingly, Toyota team members don't get to turn in an "idea" for change to their leaders; they are responsible for putting together a team, taking the right approach to studying the problem and potential solutions, piloting and getting consent from key stakeholders, and then implementing and standardizing the change. Only then can they turn in their A3 form to document their win. They must turn in completed solutions instead of just good ideas. Delegating that responsibility helps leaders to engage their workforce!

THE OPPORTUNITY MATRIX

While we haven't seen too many new Lean tools out there recently, we've created one that we find useful. It's really just a combination of existing Lean principles, but it has a hierarchy of questions to ask, so that we attack opportunities and prioritize solutions in the right order.

We call it the Opportunity Matrix, and on a wall it looks like Figure 10.

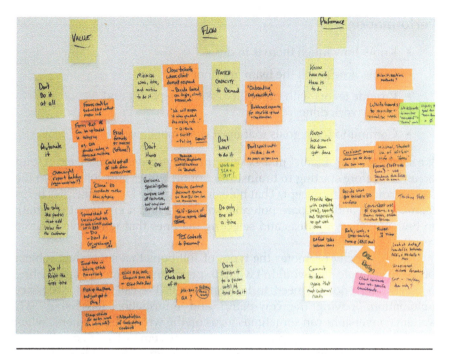

Figure 10 Opportunity Matrix example.

The lighter-colored post-its in columns under the three main-and-classic-Lean headings (Value, Flow, and Performance) are the Opportunity Matrix shell, with the following ordered hierarchy of criteria:

Value:
- Don't do it at all
- Automate it
- Do only the part(s) that add value for the customer
- Do it right the first time
- Minimize the work, time, and motion to do it
- Don't hand it off (rational specialization: the value of handoffs must outweigh the cost)
- Don't check 100% of it

Flow:
- Match capacity to demand
- Don't wait to do it
- Do only one at a time (single-piece flow)
- Don't assign it to a person until it's time to do it (transactional pull)

Performance:

- Know how much there is to do
- Know how much the team got done
- Provide teams with capability (skills), capacity, and responsibility to get work done
- Commit to team goals that meet customers' needs

We start with the "blank" matrix with the above criteria, and we put it up on a wall before starting to brainstorm opportunities and solutions in the space around each concept. That holistic view of the Lean principles helps teams to find and compare potential solutions, and it engages them both in brainstorming all ideas and selecting the ones that will drive optimal results.

The hierarchy promotes the types of solutions that solve the problem best. For example, you wouldn't want to spend time and money automating a process that doesn't need to be done at all. We call that unnecessary automation "paving the cow-path," and information technology (IT) system conversions can sometimes focus on the wrong requirements when they just copy the existing process into a new system instead of challenging it first. While a systems project should uncover non-value-added steps and streamline the business processes before automating them, we sometimes see time pressure drive some suboptimal automation.

While most of the opportunities listed in the matrix can be found in most organizations, sometimes the right solutions seem contrary to conventional wisdom. Some of the best ideas are counter-intuitive, like the example below.

FLEX WORK IN A CALL CENTER

Sometimes you can find opportunities to get creative in applying Lean Process Streamlining techniques from the Opportunity Matrix, and one new discovery for us has been in call centers. The recent prevailing theory in call center design has been to use technology and scale to create large call centers that can overcome the variation in call demand through electronic routing, predictive modeling, agent prioritization, and draconian individual accountabilities for adhering to schedules. The trouble is, even with all of that predictive data and scheduling rigor, you just can't get those pesky customers to call when they're supposed to call.

We worked with one team to find an out-of-the-box solution.

They were already doing well. The Life Administration organization at Principal Financial had been through numerous waves of change in the last six years, including process streamlining efforts that reorganized their teams, time studies to set standards for their work, and Lean Engaged Team Performance efforts that deployed visual data whiteboards and team collaborative norms to drive greater efficiency and a positive culture. They were already in the top tier of service delivery compared to life insurance industry (Life Office Management Association, "LOMA") benchmarks, and they were not-coincidentally one of the lowest-cost operations in the industry as well.

It was an excellent operation.

But then, as they say, "Change happens!"

CONTACT CENTER PRESSURE

This time, the inspiration for change came from their contact center.

The contact center hadn't been through all of the same changes, mostly because it had always been stable and well-managed, and so it hadn't attracted much attention. As part of a larger company with a strong call center planning and workforce management function, the contact center team operated with good processes, timing (Average Speed of Answer—ASA), and quality measures. It had a good call management/phone system, with the typical performance metrics available. The main efficiency measure was the same one used in call centers the world over: adherence. *Adherence* is the percentage of time that team members (called "agents") are present where they're supposed to be, when they're supposed to be there: either on a call, finishing after-call work, on a scheduled break or training segment, or "available" waiting with their phone ready to answer the next call.

The main challenge, however, was that their call center didn't have a great economy of scale. With fewer than 20 agents, the random ebbs and flows in call volume caused good hours and bad hours during the day, and there were some predictably light and heavy times even though they were varying team member schedules to try to match capacity with call demand.

You just can't make those darned customers call when they're supposed to call.

They did what they could to fill the gaps, shifting operational team members to help the call center team cover the phones during busy periods. Unfortunately, the cover time wasn't easy to predict and it disrupted the operations team members' capacity and productivity, resulting in negative impacts to their metrics and morale. It wasn't a good long-term solution.

Purposeful real-time collaboration between operations and the contact center was the answer.

FLEX WORK AND PRIORITY PROTECTION

One of the hidden opportunities in any call center is available time, those small increments that each agent has of dead time between calls. Most call centers set their call management system to give the next call to whichever agent has been off the phone the longest, resulting in a fair distribution of work among the employees.

And that guarantees that none of them have enough time in between calls to get anything else done.

Knowing that the next call could come any time, team members are accountable only for being in their seats waiting for that call, but they're not able to accomplish much else. When there are more calls than agents (called "call surplus"), it doesn't matter; everyone is on the phone all the time anyway. But during those times when there are more agents than calls ("agent surplus"), all of that available time evaporates into unproductive waiting, a minute or two at a time.

The really scary part: available time in most call centers adds up to 15-25% of total time.

So, the key to the concept of Priority Protection with Flex Work is to intentionally prioritize in the opposite way: set the priorities in the system to be *intentionally unfair*, protecting a few agents from calls until everyone else is already on the phone. Conceptually, it looks like Figure 11.

When the phones aren't fully busy, some team members know they're "first on the phone" and others know they're protected to switch over to work on operational tasks. Those protected agents keep their phones ready to answer a call too, of course, but they'll only receive a call when all of the other agents are already on the phone.

The Life Administration team implemented this concept and used the labor savings to increase call center staffing, accomplishing both goals by shifting three operations team members to the contact center and at the

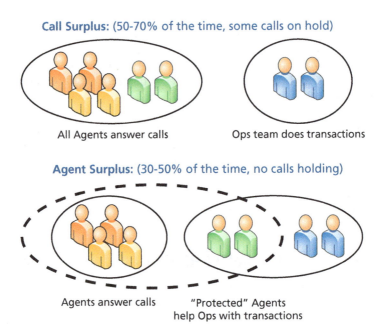

Figure 11 Call Center Priority Protection.

same time cross-training and assigning six to eight contact center team members to flex work on any given day.

The results:

- Average Speed of Answer (ASA) and Abandon Rates were cut in half.
- The majority of call agents now complete some production work during non-peak hours.
- The prioritization system is able to quickly assign staff to where the work is (calls or production work) by *moving the work rather than moving the people.*
- Improved morale and more engagement from employees – learning new skills has enabled call center agents to understand the operational work better, which has created development opportunities for the people and also allowed them to do a better job of answering calls because they now know enough to actually complete operational tasks for the customer.
- Reduced total cost per transaction.

While any change is always hard, this team has led enough change that they made it look easy. And they were still at the top of their industry benchmarks.

LEADING LEAN PROCESS STREAMLINING

As we have discussed, Step 3 in a Lean Culture transformation is to *Drive Value: Streamline the Process.*

The world is already full of books that explain the value of Lean process streamlining, so we've just included a few stories here (and a new tool, the Opportunity Matrix), and we are now ready to move on.

While the prior phases can cause pain and angst, for example by asking team members to gather time study data, they really don't cause too much fear. On the contrary, as you start to conceive, pilot, and implement real changes to the process, people will start to perceive themselves as winners and losers from the changes. As Niccolo Machiavelli wrote in *The Prince*:

> *There is nothing more difficult to carry out, nor more doubtful of success, nor more dangerous to handle, than to initiate a new order of things. For the reformer has enemies in all those who profit by the old order, and only lukewarm defenders in all those who would profit by the new order.*

While the tools are already well-documented, the key to getting started on the Lean Culture journey will be in engaging *everyone* in the organization in using those tools to improve something. Kaizen and 5S are tools that every employee can help to implement, both getting immediate results for the business and beginning to engage everyone in positive change efforts.

Here are some questions to guide leaders in Lean process streamlining:

1. Where are your "poop flags" hidden? What non-value-added work exists in your processes today? Are there handoffs that add complexity or extra work, bottlenecks that impede flow, or problems that cause rework? Do you see all of the "eight wastes" that we described in the introduction?

2. Or perhaps are your leaders and teams too close to the work to see the opportunities clearly? If so, just follow the steps: consider teaching Lean principles to your teams, creating value stream maps for their areas, and then having them compare their current state to the "vision of perfection" that they wrote in Step 1?

3. Are there inefficiencies that are hard-coded into your processes, or even driven by the design of your computer systems? How can you work around the obstacles to improve processes now, and how can you take advantage of future systems redesign opportunities to streamline processes better in the future?

4. Did (or will) your time studies highlight other opportunities that you didn't know about?

5. How will you engage your entire team in continually finding opportunities, prioritizing process change efforts, and implementing new ideas? How can Kaizen and 5S help make those activities a way of life for your teams instead of a one-time event? How will you teach your teams how to lead those types of improvement efforts, and how will you drive activity and accountability for executing them, now and forever?

In the introduction, we discussed the most common failure in Lean implementations: improving processes in the short term without transforming culture. So the most important concept to remember about Lean Process Streamlining is that you still need to do a complete Lean Culture transformation! Streamlining the process will be a very important start, but you can't stop there.

As we move on to Step 4, we'll continue that transformation by making sure the team always knows the score of the game.

4
Control the Process: Make the Work and Data Visible

If you could pick just one Lean concept, process, or performance improvement tool to apply, which one would it be?

Well of course, the answer has to be, "It depends on the situation," but think about just one.

You might think of a process map. Or the classic fishbone cause and effect diagram. Someone else might prefer the workplace organization concepts of 5S or the powerful combination of process and data in a Value Stream Map.

I'm going to say: Visual Work and Data.

VISUAL WORK AND DATA

Long ago when I worked for Coors Brewing Company, our VP of Operations made the entire leadership team read *The Great Game of Business* by Jack Stack. Stack's premise was that by sharing the numbers on a team's performance, the business becomes a game and winning becomes fun for the team. Instead of pitting "us against management," the team focuses on "us against the numbers" in a more positive way.

Applying that guidance, I created a daily scorecard for my teams and shared it with them each day, and I found that I no longer had to be the only problem-solver. The team figured out what they needed to do in order to win. My job as a leader became easier, and my team took ownership for making improvements.

In a Lean Culture of Engaged Team Performance, the team has to know how it's doing in order to care about its results.

So, while it sometimes comes in the beginning of a transformation effort and sometimes comes more near the end, there's usually a day when we put up some whiteboards in the workplace and start to write the team's numbers on them.

For each key type of work or task, we typically start by tracking daily work volumes:

- *Available work:* backlog of ready-to-work tasks that we could do today if we had time
- *Oldest date available:* an indication of how long each task waits for "first touch"
- *Pending:* work that's waiting for missing information or some other external action
- *Incoming:* the amount of work that arrived in the last 24 hours
- *Completed:* the amount of work that was done in the last 24 hours

Though we sometimes have to create an electronic version to share with dispersed teams, we find that having a physical whiteboard makes the numbers more obvious in the workplace. Anyone walking by the team's area can see their performance, and since we usually end up having the team members update the board instead of a leader, the act of updating the board daily with a dry-erase pen ensures that everyone has reviewed the team's numbers before they discuss them at their daily huddle.

A typical whiteboard looks like Figure 12 when it gets launched.

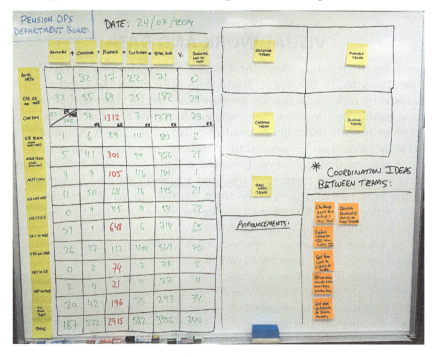

Figure 12 Example team whiteboard on Day 1.

This particular board comes from the Pension Operations team at Principal Hong Kong, and the picture was taken on the day it was deployed. Each board is tailored to measure the team's particular set of work types (listed down the left side in this picture), sometimes from a workflow system or even just counted manually. Along with the daily numbers, you can also see some other coordination items for the team on the right side of the board, as well as placeholders for some longer-term trend charts to track the movement of the key numbers over days and weeks. We'll discuss those trend charts later in this chapter, and some more-mature boards that we'll illustrate in later chapters will have those trend charts posted as well.

Incidentally, even when the team has real-time access to the numbers from a workflow system, it's still a good idea to have the team members put them up on the whiteboard every day. We sometimes hear objections to that based on the fact that people can see the numbers any time they want by just looking in the workflow system; when we ask how often they actually look at them, however, we learn that the numbers often stay out of sight and out of mind. Leaders sometimes have to insist on the teams using visual whiteboards for a while, until updating the whiteboard becomes a habit.

This example board has a few additional work status types compared to the short list we made above, including available, checking, pending, and suspended work types, which all combine to form the total work count in their workflow system. This team had substantial quantities of work in each of those columns, so we amended the typical list to include more types of work.

It's important to be able to segregate the work into these different types, mostly because some types are controllable in different ways compared to others. For example, Available work belongs to the team, but Pending is probably in the hands of another team or even a customer, while Checking may belong to a quality control group. This particular team even had a special Suspended status for work that was never expected to come back from a customer, but they kept it on the board because the company had a regulatory requirement to continue to track it.

One very interesting relationship involves available work (i.e., the new backlog in available status) and total work (total backlog of work in process in all status types) in comparison to the rate of incoming work (the mathematical inverse of another Lean metric, the "takt," or time between arrivals of one unit of work demand). According to Little's Law, an easy way to estimate the typical turnaround time of the work (in business days) is to divide the available work by the incoming rate in the last 24-hour workday (see Figure 13).

Total work:	60 units
Arrival rate of work:	15 units/day
Days of inventory:	= 4 days
Available work:	30 units
Arrival rate of work:	15 units/day
Days of available inventory:	= 2 days

Figure 13 Turnaround time estimation.

In the above example, if we have 60 units of work in total in the various status types, and if we receive 15 units per day of incoming work, we can expect that the average turnaround time is 60/15 = 4 days. If 30 of those 60 units are in Available status, then 30/15 = 2 days of inventory units are waiting for their first touch. The team has to learn how to do those quick calculations on their whiteboards and in their heads, because when we proceed to the next two steps in the transformation process (*Organize the Team* and *Set Team Goals*), we will right-size each team for their workflow, and then one of the key team goals will be to keep available work at 1-2 days or less (for most teams).

Once we deploy the whiteboards, we ask the team to conduct a 5-minute huddle around them at least once a day. The huddle becomes a time for the team to discuss the plan for the day, shift priorities or resources, and discuss ideas for improvement. Most importantly, it lets the team take ownership for the work. And as they start using their whiteboard to collaborate, we quickly start to see the team work down the available and pending counts, communicate better to share work and resources, and look for new ways to improve performance. They become engaged.

The whiteboard works every time.

COLLABORATIVE NORMS

Collaborative norms are ways that teams work together, guidelines or "rules of the road" that people use to get along and get work done. Deploying a whiteboard can be a trigger for adjusting other norms that optimize performance, starting with the team huddles that we've described above.

Believe it or not, it takes great self-discipline to do a five-minute team huddle. Sometimes the first huddle takes 45 minutes instead of just five. The challenge is that it can take a while for people to learn the right amount of depth to take the conversations; the huddle shouldn't take the place of the weekly team meeting, and it can't be used to solve complex problems. Teams should just use their huddles to coordinate daily plans and *identify* problems, then delegate responsibility to sub-teams (using Kaizen) to resolve issues in separate discussions.

Teams should adopt other specific collaborative norms to support the self-discipline they need. One example: Menlo Innovations uses a Viking helmet to control behavior during their huddles. Only the person holding the helmet may speak, and the helmet has to be passed around in sequence to everyone. If Menlo can do a full 50-person company meeting every day with the helmet in 13 minutes, most typical teams should be able to execute a huddle in 5 minutes.

Collaborative norms aren't just about meetings and huddles, however. Good teams use many different types of collaborative norms to drive self-discipline in communication and daily interaction. David Marquet tells a number of stories about collaborative norms in his book, *Turn the Ship Around!* When creating mapping charts of the ocean for their submarine operations, he discovered that different teams were using different colors on the charts they made. He explains:

> *I wanted the colors to be consistent and convey information. Someone suggested that we use…shades of red [to] represent shallow water [and] shades of blue to represent deeper water. We also came up with standard schemes for water assignments. [Our ship's] water would always be blue in military exercises; other [friendly] submarines would be yellow; areas where we shared water and were separated by depth zone would be – you guessed it – green!*

Though he doesn't intentionally call out collaborative norms as a separate concept, Marquet filled his book with stories where his teams figured out good ways to do things and then hard-coded them into their culture by setting norms around executing those processes the same way every time. Some other examples included:

- *The way people talked to each other:* instead of asking permission to do things, sailors would say, "I intend to do X, Y, and Z," and the captain would just say, "Very well." This norm encouraged initiative and empowered people to think instead of waiting to be told what to do. A simple collaborative norm created a Sea Change in thinking.

- *Where people slept:* when damage occurs to a submarine, sailors who are off-shift have to take care of fire-fighting and damage-control responsibilities so that the on-shift crew can continue running the ship. In the past, sleeping arrangements had been selected based on rank and privilege, but the crew changed assignments to put everyone's berth as close as possible to their assigned damage control stations. Not only was this more efficient, but it sent a message: the capability for the whole team to survive is more important than giving the ranking team members the most comfortable spots.

- *Accountability:* every operation, from large to tiny, always designated a "Chief in Charge" to clarify accountability and leadership roles.

Simple collaborative norms allow clarity of communication, prevent mistakes, encourage teamwork, and streamline work. Leaders and teams have to intentionally design those norms, then enforce self-discipline of using them properly every time.

The whiteboard is a great place to start, and it can become a focal point for that collaboration when the team huddles around it to share information, but look for other norms to set as well.

ROLLING WHITEBOARDS ARE EXPENSIVE!

Even though most organizations already have some whiteboards hanging in conference rooms, a new large whiteboard with wheels provides some flexibility, since we can pilot it with a team and then decide where it fits best in their work area as they start to use it. We want the team to do the huddle out in their work area, not in a conference room. Unfortunately, that wheeled version of a whiteboard can be expensive; we've seen them cost $400-800 each.

One senior leader, now a great friend of mine, wasn't so sure she wanted to buy them when we first discussed the concept. We had recently worked together to transform her team's processes, and we had found some backlog issues on two of her newly reorganized teams. We needed the visual data to allow the teams to collaborate better to reduce the backlog, both inside each team and between the two teams, and we didn't have much time to debate the purchase. But paying more than $1,000 for a couple of whiteboards seemed like such a waste.

I suggested, "How about you buy them now and start the team huddles, and when I come back in a few weeks to check on progress, we can decide if the whiteboards are useful enough. If you don't want to keep them, I'll take them to another client and you can deduct the cost from one of our invoices. Would that work?" It was my first time underwriting consigned equipment, but I was confident—the whiteboards always work.

They bought the boards and started using them.

When I returned to their city a few weeks later, I made sure that my rental car that week was a pickup truck, and when I first saw the leader, I said, "I brought a pickup truck this week."

"Why?" she asked. She had forgotten already.

"To get the whiteboards," I replied. "Our other client downtown will take them." I hadn't really talked to the other client about it yet…

She quietly left the office and went out to the work floor, and I followed her out there and found her hugging one of the boards. She was keeping them.

TREND CHARTS

One key concept of measurement is that *anything worth measuring is probably worth viewing on a chart trended over time*. In his fairly short and really insightful book, *Understanding Variation,* Donald Wheeler made a strong and commonsense case for using past data trends to understand the context of the current data point in order to know how to react. That's a core concept called "Special Cause and Common Cause" variation, and it's been around for almost a century as a component of quality control theory.

In addition to the daily numbers on the whiteboard that help the team devise their daily plan, therefore, we also want to see if those numbers are trending up, down, or "in control" (randomly varying about the average, but not shifting or trending in a non-random way). So we make trend charts with historical data using those same daily numbers and display the team's performance over time.

The chart in Figure 14 is an example from Jennifer Wilson's transformation of Ecova's Expense Data Management team. This chart was owned by the Financial Services Pilot Team that was formed to test a new way of organization, and in later chapters we'll talk about the reorganization that occurred on that team. In this case, the team decided to put available work and the daily completion rate on the same chart, so that they could compare those two very-different measurements visually. They also allowed the Excel software to add trend lines to help the team see their progress.

As you can see, when the team started tracking their daily data, the total Available inventory was 3,000 units and the daily Completion rate was about 750 per day. Using the turnaround time estimation method that we discussed earlier in this chapter, you can see that 3,000/750 = 4 days, and so the available work was waiting quite a while before being touched. This resulted in many of the typical wastes of backlog that we've already discussed, including extra prioritization, expediting work, additional client follow-up questions, and duplicate requests.

The team knew that one of the keys to improving their performance would be to reduce the turnaround time by cutting the backlog. Seeing this chart on the whiteboard with their daily numbers on it, even though they varied a bit day-to-day, helped the team to envision their goal and monitor their progress.

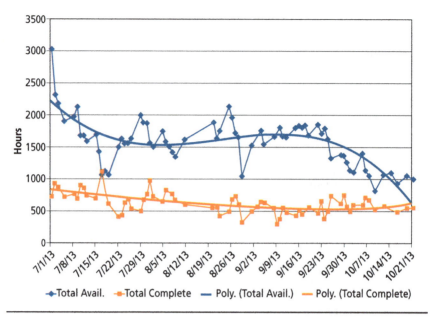

Figure 14   Available and completed work trended over time.

Three months later, in early October, their available work was down to 1,000 units and their completion rate was 600 per day. The same estimation method confirms that their turnaround time was now reduced to 1-2 days.

FREEDOM THROUGH TYRANNY

The whole idea of visual work and data is to let the work manage the people, which creates a much more positive environment than the traditional approach of supervisors managing the people. By allowing teams to see their work, plan how to get it done, and take pride in completing it, we transfer accountability from leadership to everyone.

It's actually liberating!

Rich Sheridan calls this "freedom through tyranny" in *Joy, Inc.* He explains:

> *The beautiful part of… [the] Menlo visual displays is that there is no ambiguity. Each [team] knows which project it is assigned to this week and what its work plan is for the next five days. It is complete and total tyranny. This may be a funny statement for one of the world's most democratic companies, I know. But this is where the freedom of our culture really kicks in. The [teams] can pursue the work they love without someone hanging over their shoulder asking, "How's it going? Whatcha working on?" We don't need that guy.*

It's equally liberating for leaders. In *Building Engaged Team Performance*, we recounted the story of a tour that illustrated the benefits for leaders of an evolved Lean Culture:

> *In 2008, we had the great fortune to bring another team that was starting a new performance transformation project on a tour of the GPS [Group Proposal Services] team. Coincidentally, one of the former leaders of the new project's department had recently been transferred to the GPS and was our tour guide. So, all the leaders in the new project's department knew her and trusted her, and she knew the challenges that they faced because she used to work with all of them. After hearing her enthusiastic description of the process and the metrics during the tour, one of them asked her a great question: "So, what's different about your job now?"*
>
> *Initially, she scared them by saying, "Well, you might think this is a bad thing, but I spend a half hour every morning to make sure the metrics are posted and the team sees them. We have a team huddle to discuss the current status, yesterday's performance, and any special situations."*
>
> *Heads nodded. One person commented, "Yeah, we'd never have the extra time to do that data work." Just for a moment, I was worried.*
>
> *But then the tour guide-leader said, "And after that, I don't have to do anything special to make sure the work gets done. I don't have to check to make sure people are working. I don't have to move resources around. I don't have to babysit anything or anybody. The team takes care of the work. You know me, and I know what you have to deal with in your department, because I used to work with you. The difference is that I spend a half hour on the metrics and then I get to be proactive all day. I get to spend the day doing my job, interacting with our customers and developing people."*
>
> *Wow!*

LEADING VISUAL DATA AND INTEGRATING THE NEXT STEPS

In this chapter, *Control the Process: Make the Work and Data Visible*, we've discussed the importance of deploying whiteboards and trends charts to help the team see their performance and engage in their work.

As David Marquet echoes in *Turn the Ship Around!*, "Simply providing the data to the teams on their relative performance results in a natural desire to improve." Making the business a game as Jack Stack suggested decades ago has now come to be called "gamification," and it is the easiest step in the process so far. It's also the most critically important.

As a leader, ask yourself:

1. How can you encourage the real-time sharing of performance data so that teams can see where they are, where they've been, and where they need to go? You may have to mandate a daily team huddle for a while, until everyone sees the value in it.
2. What resources will you need to automate systems and data reporting processes so that those numbers are available to the people who need to see them in real time?
3. How can you share the data with teams, particularly those that have dispersed team members or other geographic challenges?
4. How will you get teams to take ownership for their numbers? If they see the purpose as just reporting their status to senior leaders, they'll miss the opportunity to engage fully in owning their outcomes.
5. What other collaborative norms can you set and impose self-discipline to leverage?

As you'll see in the next few chapters, a number of the next steps really go together. In particular, Step 4 (*Control the Process: Make Work and Data Visible*) enables the next three steps of our transformation approach, which really can happen concurrently:

- Step 5, *Transform: Organize the Team*
- Step 6, *Engage! Set Team Goals*
- Step 7, *Implement Change: Lead the Transition*

We'll have to explain the steps one at a time over the next few chapters, but the visual display of whiteboard data is really a key to getting started on all of them at once. When we proceed to Step 5, you'll see that organizing the team is another data-based adventure, using both Lean Culture principles and time study data to model the right size team for the work. And then Step 6 leverages the whiteboard to set a goal for keeping up with the workflow for the team as whole. In Step 7, we expand the change across the whole organization and reinforce the collaborative norms that each team needs for communication and self-direction.

Onward!

5

Transform: Organize the Team

We'll now return to Ecova's Lean Culture transformation, which started with the initial time study that Jennifer Wilson's Expense Data Management team deployed in a previous chapter. They were Ecova's first team to go through the transformation approach. We've already discussed their time study results and the strongly committed leadership there, but we'll start here with a bit more about their situation.

A FUNCTIONAL ORGANIZATION

The company's size had grown substantially in the last two years. Business was booming, and a functional organization had helped to enable that growth, with narrowly defined roles that allowed incremental hiring and training to maintain and scale their operational capacity. It made perfect sense at the time, but it wasn't very Lean.

The typical process had five touches to accomplish the main result of paying a utility bill for a client (which included mail scanning, data entry, financial edit analysis, consumption edit analysis, and payment authorization). There were also other roles that specialized in customer service and managing specific vendor issues. It wasn't unusual for a piece of work to touch seven or eight people before being completed, and each role was staffed with well-trained experts in large functional teams. The process map (pictured in Figure 15) had a lot of steps.

But with all of those roles and handoffs, there were inefficiencies as well, some of which we've already discussed in previous chapters. Upstream data entry errors propagated to roles down the line, so people in those roles felt the need to check for them, and there was quite a bit of duplication of effort when different people looked at the same work item to do slightly different actions (but had to read the same basic records and data to accomplish their tasks).

Figure 15 Ecova energy data management process.

Even worse, the strict role definition created a "not my job" feeling for some of the people, who didn't feel empowered or accountable to finish work that belonged to other roles. That lack of empowerment also created some divisions among the people and teams, with tensions occasionally developing between employees.

Jennifer Wilson recalls:

> *For the functional roles, we were able to create standards for each person to follow that were specific to the process, but it insulated many roles from the customer. People didn't think outside of their own role or have the internal and external client in mind if they weren't interacting with them on a daily basis. It was more of a silo approach instead of an end-to-end process.*
>
> *Individual team members didn't have visibility to key questions: Where does my work go next? Who is impacted? What is the expected outcome?*
>
> *The organizational structure really created an "us vs. them" mentality between the operational group and client-facing teams, and even within the operational groups themselves. When we tried to track down an*

> issue and find the root cause, we had to go to several functional roles to pinpoint what happened and then heard most of them say, "That isn't my job; it belongs to them." It was frustrating to have to go to several different functional teams make changes for a specific client.

The functional organization worked, but it didn't work perfectly.

CUSTOMER-FOCUSED TEAMS

We often find opportunities to reorganize teams to focus on specific sets of customers. Our customers drive our purpose, and so organizing around customer groups allows team members to get closer to customers and see the team's impacts on customers more clearly. We call that gaining "line of sight" to the customer.

The Lean transformation team decided to pilot a change that impacted both the process and the organization, using data from their time study to right-size two cross-functional teams that combined multiple roles with a focus on a vertical grouping of customers. Instead of a large functional organization with each type of work on a separate team, in the new organization each 10- to 15-person team had all of the functions represented on it, and the people were encouraged to collaborate among all roles to get the work done for their specific vertical group of customers.

The teams were small enough for team members to feel connected to each other and the customer, while large enough in scale to overcome the variation in workflow encountered by various roles. In order to make that scalability work, though, we had to redesign the team's collaborative norms around their work. As you recall from a previous chapter, collaborative norms are the internal agreements that a team makes among team members, defining who's going to do what work and how the team members will help each other get it all done.

In *Joy, Inc.*, Rich Sheridan describes collaborative norms as the self-discipline beneath the surface of a great organization. He explains:

> Heroes rely on risky heroics. Great teams rely on discipline.... The rigor and discipline that exist just an inch below the surface of what you see at Menlo [have] led to unprecedented quality in our products.... No one at Menlo (including me) can ever say, "Well, this task that just came up is really important and we don't have time to use our process." It would actually take us more time to not use our process. At Menlo, we are all held accountable to our process. We believe in that process. We know it produces quality results.

At Ecova, we had to create new collaborative norms that aligned with the new processes, measures, and visual data. Team members were asked to do as much as they could on each work item rather than passing it off to another role as they had in the past, with a few exceptions where those handoffs were still rationalized by economies of scale. Team members had to change from the "my work and your work" attitudes of the prior functional roles, and work toward an "our work" view. Of course, leaders had to give the team members training to facilitate that cross-functionality.

We started with a pilot of the new organizational concept on two teams organized across two key customer vertical groups—Financial Services and Pipelines. The teams wanted to learn from the pilots, but they also wanted the pilots to help prove to the company as a whole that the new way of organizing was going to work, so they picked two very different customer groupings to pilot.

In order to design the pilot teams with the right number of resources (roles of each type) for the work that their group of clients would be sending, we first had to create mathematical models from the time study data. A few VLOOKUP and PIVOT TABLE commands in Excel later, we had aggregated the time study data by customer grouping and had modeled the number of team members of each role type that we would need to support each group of customers. We used the time study data to add up the time all team members spent on those actual clients, and then we applied a standard workday of 6.5 hours of work per day present on-site, reduced by personal-time-off (PTO) and sick day planning factors. We eventually expected 5.5 hours of work per paid 8-hour day.

We also used a multiple regression analysis to create a predictive staffing model for adding new clients to the teams' workload, finding a few client attributes that correlated with the majority of the variation in work. What we found, of course, is that not all clients were equal. The mathematical modeling became critical in designing the optimal team sizes, replacing the "one for you, one for me" equal distribution of clients with a much more accurate workload model.

Perhaps obviously, the opportunity to run a pilot is also an opportunity to right-size teams. In a previous chapter, we shared the team performance data from this same organization prior to their transformation, showing that some functional teams were working more hours per day than others, and we explained carefully that this was not the employees' fault. Teams that are under-sized for their workload can't keep up, and teams that are over-sized for their workload can't be efficient. So the chance to change the team structure is also an opportunity to put just the right amount of labor there to support those customers, if you have a data-based model for figuring out that workload from a time study.

We did!

LAUNCHING THE PILOTS

We launched the pilots with some fanfare, moving the people from various roles to sit together on the two new teams. We chose a spot for each of the two teams on different floors of the building, so that others could walk by and see what was going on. Everyone was interested to see how the pilots would go, and of course there were some differences of opinion about whether the new design would work or not.

We shared the trend chart in the previous chapter that demonstrated the backlog reduction that we began to immediately see. Everyone knew that was a good thing. The most important tool to deploy at the beginning, of course, was a whiteboard.

The whiteboards for each team displayed the daily work available, pending, and completed, which allowed for coordination of resources and provided a communication medium for team members to plan the team's workday together. You'll also recognize the trend chart in the bottom-left of the board, since we shared that in the previous chapter.

We selected a team leader for each of the two teams, and both of them did a fantastic job of facilitating huddle discussions and work prioritization each day. They challenged their teams to work together to get all of the work done, particularly in sharing work among different roles. One of the leaders was a Client Service Representative at the beginning of the change effort and ended up as a manager two years later. She was both originally selected to lead her peers and later promoted because of her knack for getting the team to buy in to change.

The note at the top-right corner of Figure 16 is a particularly positive illustration of her impact on the team. "It's not my job? Yes, yes it is!" Leadership matters.

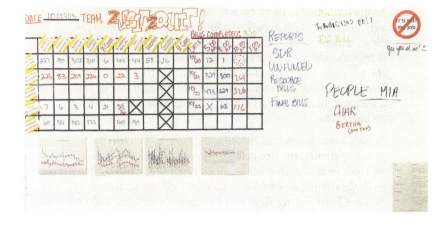

Figure 16 Ecova customer-focused team whiteboard.

PILOT RESULTS

A few weeks into the pilot, David Cline, the executive leading the deployment of the new Lean Culture (which now had a name—the Ecova Management System), came back with me to talk with the two pilot teams. We asked the pilot team members, "What's different?"

While the responses weren't really surprising, we saw the most positive Lean Culture benefit up front—the team understood and were applying Lean principles. One person explained:

> *My role is an account specialist, and one of my assigned responsibilities is in dealing with what we call 'bills late arriving,' where our computer system has us go look for a bill that's missing. This is a really good service that we offer our clients, because sometimes a utility bill could get lost in the mail and cause a late charge if we didn't know to go and look for it. Anyway, I start by making a call to the utility to see where the bill is, but sometimes I need to call the client as well. In the old organization, it was possible for me to get any client's work, and so I didn't know all of those hundreds of clients personally.*
>
> *Consequently, the Client Service Representatives [another role] didn't want dozens of us all calling and emailing their clients, since the clients might get a handful of different calls from different Ecova employees throughout the day and get confused about whom to call back. So we had to hand off our questions to the assigned Client Service Rep for each client and then wait for an answer, which might take a day or two. I sometimes had to check back to see if the answer was there yet, and I had to keep track of which Reps owed me answers about which clients. Not only was it extra work for me, but it was also slower for the client to get their bill. And then if the bill came late, we had to call the utility again to get the late fee reversed. The extra handoffs and waiting just caused a snowball of work to roll down the mountain and become an avalanche.*
>
> *Now it's much different. Because we only work with one group of clients, the two account specialist roles on our team sit right next to each other so we can coordinate our contacts with the clients, and we know all of our clients now anyway. So the Client Service Reps and the clients are happy to let us just coordinate with the clients directly instead of having to hand the questions back and forth. That saves us time, gets the work done better and faster for the clients, and lets the Client Service Reps work on other important things.*

The team members not only supported the changes; they understood the Lean principles that formed the foundation of the new organization. Client focus had reduced the need for the non-value-added work of managing all of the handoffs between functional teams. Sometimes that internal coordination work is invisible, buried in a workflow system, and you don't really see the benefits of changing until you pilot something new.

Similar to the example above, team members were able to translate the benefits of the new organizational design into positive impacts on the customer, including:

- Reduction of backlog and quicker response time to questions
- More insightful answers because the Ecova operational teams have increased individual knowledge of the client and related vertical industry
- Quicker throughput of bills, which improved and maintained low late fees
- Improved analysis of the bills, with more insightful findings and improved data accuracy
- Clients continue to have a Client Service Representative as their primary point of contact for program related questions or needs

Not only was that streamlined organization better for the clients, however. It was also better for the employees. Feeling empowered to get things done instead of passing work around, the team members felt a greater connection to the customer and the business. They knew where they stood every day by looking at the data on their whiteboard, and they were empowered and expected to collaborate to get everything done. We'll talk more about that concept as we introduce team goals in the next chapter as well.

Finally, at the end of our pilot reviews with the teams, David and I had another of those moments where we played with the teams a little, telling them, "Thanks for participating in the pilot. Are you ready to go back to your functional teams while we assess the results and decide what to do?"

There were a few incredulous looks on team members' faces until they realized we were kidding.

One team member confirmed out loud the way they all felt, "We are not going back."

ORGANIZING THE WHOLE DEPARTMENT

In Step 5, *Transform: Organize the Team*, we have built upon the time study and process analysis in Step 2, the process streamlining of Step 3, and the visual data boards and trend charts that we had designed in Step 4, leveraging all of that work to make a dramatic change to the design of the organization to align its workflow with its customers.

After piloting the concept to build support for the changes, the department then expanded that pilot to conduct a full reorganization of all teams. We had to do more mathematical modeling to design each team with the right size for the work in their customer group, and then the executive team had to reorganize the department's leadership team to align with the new team structure, cross-train roles as appropriate, move team members into co-located areas, and buy 16 more whiteboards.

Cross-training usually turns out to be a critical enabler of both the new organization design and the collaborative norms that are necessary to share work and deliver results as a team instead of a group of individuals. Additional knowledge also drives better employee engagement by giving people a broader perspective and confidence in making decisions. As David Marquet says, "As authority is delegated, technical knowledge at all levels takes on a greater importance… If all you need to do is what you're told, then you don't need to understand your craft. However, as your ability to make decisions increases, then you need intimate technical knowledge on which to base those decisions."

Engagement enables personal growth, and personal growth enables engagement.

While preparing the organization and transitioning to a new team structure was a lot of work and took a number of months, the pilots helped the whole group buy in to the goal of organizing differently to do the work better, satisfy clients, and engage employees. Over time, Ecova saw the following benefits of the client-focused teams:

- Focuses teams on customer verticals, allowing teams to become expert at industry norms.
- Team members have become more knowledgeable, efficient, and effective.
- "One touch" approach reduces handoffs and escalated issues.
- Clients have a knowledgeable small team supporting them, in addition to a primary contact.
- Each team has a team leader focused on meeting client expectations, developing employees, and managing and measuring the processes, rather than managing a narrow function.

Jennifer Wilson remembers how that transition felt:

> *In the beginning of this process I could see how my leaders reacted to what was going on, and I appreciated the ones who jumped right in to support the effort.*

> There was one leader in particular I was worried would not fully support the effort to move into vertical teams. As we moved through the process, that leader turned out to be one of the biggest advocates and became one to watch. He believed in the new role and wanted to own an industry team, encouraged the employees, and created a team environment that was truly remarkable.
>
> We found that we could still have standards by function but also focus on an industry-specific group of clients and their individual needs. The employees felt more connected to their work. They started understanding the industry groupings and the clients they supported each day, learning the specific needs of each client. There were celebrations by team, goals created and met, and a team atmosphere that increased the overall production and reduced the handoffs.
>
> From the overall restructuring of the department from functional to vertical teams, including impacts from the reduction in handoffs, increased alignment with our clients, and better employee engagement, we were able to save the company over $1.4 million annually.
>
> It felt wonderful to be able to move such a large group in a new direction and have backing for the change at all levels throughout the organization.

All of that was starting to feel like a Lean Culture of Engaged Team Performance. It was an exciting time for them, but they weren't done quite yet.

LEADING THE TRANSFORMATION: ORGANIZE THE TEAM

As you've seen, the benefits of organizing the team around groups of customers can include greater efficiency through handoff reduction, stronger relationship development with customers, and better line of sight for employees to the outcomes they're delivering. Almost as important, an additional benefit of the organizational transformation is the opportunity to right-size the team.

A right-sized team can use its work to manage its people by reorienting everyone on just getting work done, because they have just enough capacity. We almost called this step "Reorganize the Team," but we intentionally left off the "re" prefix because people the world over fear the word "reorg" so greatly. Employees see a reorganization as an event where people lose their jobs. They think that a reorganization is an evil plot hatched by senior leaders in a smoke-filled room somewhere in the HR department's area or an off-site conference center. Sometimes they're right.

But again, it doesn't have to be that way. As you pilot a new organization, you certainly have to move people to new roles, but leaders who take a long-term view of the business will see the cultural benefits of leading these changes in a humane way. By finding additional work, cross-training, and short-term projects for displaced people while they wait for attrition and/or growth to rebalance staffing levels, leaders can prevent involuntary departures and protect all of the people, while still moving the organization forward. This works very well as long as you're not in a hurry, and the way to give yourself enough time is to start on the path to change now.

The best organization changes we've seen have resulted from Lean Culture transformations where employees generated ideas like Customer Focused Teams and executed pilots to prove that they worked. As in the Ecova story, once they experienced the value of the new process and organization, employees didn't want to go back.

As a leader, you have to create the conditions for that buy-in, and the best way to do that is to engage employees all along the way in designing the solution and give them the authority to try it even if you're not sure that it will work. Here are some questions you can ask yourself:

1. Are you willing to consider changing the organization to match the process and focus on the customer? If you have to change customer assignments, how can you articulate or demonstrate to the customers that the new organization will better serve their needs?

2. You just had a reorg on _____ (fill in the blank)—everyone's done one recently! How does it make your leadership team look if you change the organization yet again? Does it mean that your previous versions were wrong, or was that just part of the necessary evolution of your business? How can the changes be viewed positively?

3. Which mid-level leaders will resist the changes when they lose power, scope, or influence? What new roles, opportunities, or exit plans can you offer them?

4. How can you engage a team in piloting a new organization, learning from that pilot, and then making changes to allow a stronger final design?

People learn by winning and win by learning, and the best organization will be able to get the right work done right (effectively), with just enough resources (efficiently). Employees don't want boring jobs where they can coast every day; they want challenging roles where they can contribute to a winning team, a sustainable team that grows by delivering great products and services for customers.

And then they need goals to match. And so we go on to Step 6, *Engage! Set Team Goals.*

6

Engage!
Set Team Goals

Just as the Ecova team was transforming its organization, a team at Principal Financial was embarking on a similar journey.

THE TEAM'S MISSION

When the Annuities Operations team at Principal Financial started their Lean Engaged Team Performance transformation in 2012, their mission was clear: to make their processes more scalable in order to be able to expand production in the event of a volume spike. They had experienced a dramatic volume increase a few years before, and the pain from that event had built the commitment for change for their team.

They just didn't know exactly how they were going to accomplish that mission.

So their team went through the Lean Engaged Team Performance transformation steps, analyzing their business processes and conducting a time study to understand the workflow, then modeling the labor required for the various task types. And we learned some interesting things:

- Handoffs and role differentiation in the process that had been implemented in the last few years to improve short-term scalability had actually done the opposite in the long run, creating barriers to cross-functional work and increasing total work time needed to complete the tasks.

- While New Business work was being accomplished quickly, backlogs in some other types of "Administrative" work were creating more work (like duplicates, status checks, expediting work, etc.) and consuming team time; even worse, it felt to the team members as though they were always living on the edge of their deadlines.

- Their teams were working hard, but their performance was being driven and yet also limited by individual goals; they were missing opportunities to collaborate to get more work done as a team.

Many teams learn to live with significant backlogs, and many teams just like this one make promises of 2- to 5-day turnaround times that seem reasonable to their customers. But when we measure the work, we often find that the work time per task is only 15-30 minutes. Quite often, a 30-minute task doesn't really take 5 days to complete; it just waits until day 4 to get started. And then for reasons we've discussed already, the backlog itself creates extra work.

While those observations certainly challenged a number of paradigms, the leaders and their teams were willing to try the ideas that their transformation team proposed, and we identified some ways to deploy visual work controls and reorganize with fewer roles. As the process changes generated a bit of extra capacity to get more work done, the project leaders unveiled a much more substantial change. We set a new team goal that came to be called "Mission 24."

They were about to revolutionize their culture!

MISSION 24

The new mission: *get all work done within 24 hours of arrival* (if the work arrives in good order).

While some people challenged that idea as potentially over-servicing the customer, getting work done before it was expected, the team soon realized the counterintuitive truth that *getting rid of backlogs is actually cheaper*. There are a lot of bad things that can happen as backlogged items age in the work queue. The team members knew that the backlogs caused them to receive duplicate tasks, questions about work status, and requests to expedite work.

Nevertheless, it took a little while to convince everyone that work that arrived today should be done today. The teams had to work down their significant backlogs slowly over time, but we started simply by showing them the numbers and having a daily huddle to monitor progress. By now you won't be surprised to learn that they put the numbers on a whiteboard, as shown in Figure 17.

The chart shows the quantities of tasks currently waiting in the triage, process, and follow-up queues (labeled T, P, and F), as well as the counts on the previous day (the column under the date 4/6). The team members were able to see where the work was, observe whether queues were increasing or shrinking, and decide how to collaborate to get more work done.

As the backlogs of work melted away, the team saw the other key benefit of staying within 24 hours on everything: if they ever did get another volume spike, there wouldn't be many other items already in the work queues to get in the way.

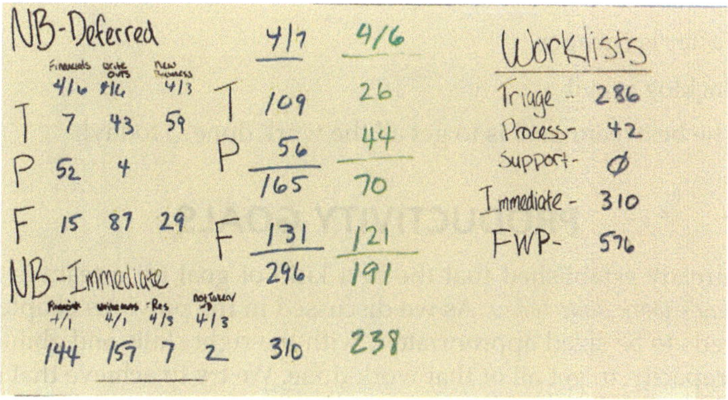

Engage! Set Team Goals 83

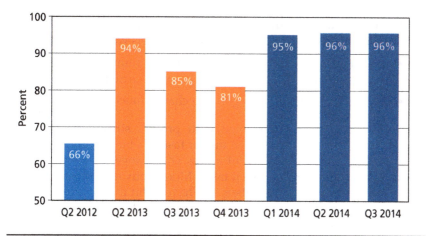

Figure 17 Principal Annuities daily whiteboard.

Mission Accomplished!

After more than a year of work to change processes, cross-train team members, and work down the queues, they accomplished their Mission 24 in mid-2013. Figure 18 shows their dramatic change in performance.

Then right after that, they finally did get the volume spike in mid-2013 that they had always feared would come again, and *it was a non-event*. They were able to take on the additional volumes and grow their queues moderately while still meeting due dates better than during "normal" times in the past. They then scaled up their staffing levels with strong training processes and worked the backlogs back down to meet their Mission 24 goal again in 2014.

Their new culture and team goals got them through it unscathed.

Figure 18 Percent of work completed in 24 hours.

All of this reinforces some important conclusions:
- Faster is cheaper.
- Backlog is evil.
- The best team goal is to get all the work done… today!

PRODUCTIVITY GOALS

We've already established that the best kind of goal for a team is to *get all of today's work done today*. As we discussed in the previous chapter, the team needs to be sized appropriately, with the right skills and abilities as well as capacity, to get all of that work done. We try to achieve that right-sizing in the previous Step 5 *(Transform: Organize the Team)* using data models from our time study. So by the time we reach Step 6, we should have the right sized team with the right skills, and we're able to set a team goal of getting the work done every day.

Have you ever seen teams, though, that had *productivity goals* instead? This would look like some kind of count or volume that team members are supposed to complete daily, weekly, or monthly. These goals are set with the best of intentions, hoping to stretch or motivate the team to get more done, but they often have the opposite effect.

While individual goals can affect behavior with a variety of positive and negative impacts, productivity goals don't motivate teams much at all. It's hard to build a positive vision for the statement, "Let's get more work done today than we did yesterday." The team has a hard time connecting that goal to a positive outcome. The reward for hitting that goal will just be… more work expected tomorrow. So this concept of the stretch goal is actually another hindrance for productivity, because it creates an "us against them" relationship challenge between the employees and management.

The count-based productivity goal only impacts behavior when the team is close to achieving it anyway. Think of it this way:
- Each item of work takes a certain amount of time to accomplish, which we measured during the time study in Step 2.
- That amount of time isn't going to change much based on a goal.

The time work takes could change with process streamlining or new technology, or perhaps a different mix of task attributes (product, client, or other work type variables). But unless you change the process or the work itself, it takes the time that it takes. More motivation doesn't make a task go much faster; team members still have to hit the same keys on the computer and enter the same information, regardless of how motivated they feel that day.

So the question is really whether the team has the time (capacity) to do the work (meet the demand) or not, given the standard time to complete each item. There are three options:

1. If the team is barely sized to hit the goal, the goal will motivate them to get the work done. Great!
2. If the team isn't sized with enough capacity to get all of the work done, they can't hit the goal anyway. The goal will just frustrate the team by seeming to be out of reach.
3. If the team is over-sized with too much capacity, they can hit the goal without being efficient. In that case, the goal really isn't positively impacting behavior.

And whose job is it to give the team enough capacity to hit the goal? Yes, that's the leadership's job.

This all leads to one simple conclusion: the only time the productivity goal is appropriate is when the team is just the right size, and if so, *a much simpler goal will work* and will feel much more connected to the customer for the team anyway: we'll go back to the goal of "just get all the work done today."

INDIVIDUAL GOALS

Even worse, sometimes organizations distribute those team productivity goals by splitting them up into individual goals. That's like telling the starting five players on a basketball team, "The team will win if each of you individually scores 20 points tonight." If each of them scores 20, the team will score 100 and will probably win, right?

Wrong.

What typically happens when you set all individual goals is not winning:

- Team members focus on scoring their own points instead of assisting others or playing defense.
- A team member could slack off a little once he or she hits his or her 20-point goal.
- Invariably, a few people hit the goal, a few miss it, and the team loses.

That's why good basketball teams don't focus on individual goals, except maybe during All-Star Games where the outcome doesn't matter. And that's why hockey teams count a point for each individual who scores as well as up to two players who assist on a goal. The best individual indicator of hockey performance is plus/minus, actually a team measurement that has a sum of all the goals scored while each player was on the ice, offsetting points for and against the team. The individuals are measured on a team outcome. Hockey is a team sport.

"Just about every sport is in some sense a team sport," says Carol Dweck in *Mindset*. "No one does it alone. Even in individual sports, like tennis or golf, great athletes have a team—coaches, trainers, caddies, managers, mentors."

Dweck quotes John Wooden, the legendary UCLA basketball coach, who explained why he opposed retiring the jerseys of some of his greatest players, including Kareem Abdul-Jabbar and Bill Walton: "Other fellows who played on our team also wore those numbers. Some of those players gave me close to everything they had.... The jersey and the number on it never belong to just one single player, no matter how great or how big a 'star' that particular player is. It goes against the concept of what a team is."

Jim Knight, "rock star" public speaker and former global training leader at Hard Rock International, says, "Individual agendas produce random actions. In other words, if employees don't share a collective vision of the brand, they will produce dysfunctional team results. In the absence of a shared purpose, even the best employees will contribute to an eventual culture of confusion."

Knight continues: "On the flipside, a shared mindset produces aligned actions. In following the successes of Fortune 500 companies, aside from the fact they make more money and command more market share than their competitors, I see that they communicate like crazy with their internal bases, maintaining a strong sense of transparency and ultimately loyalty. In these high-performing organizations, everyone knows the mission. Every front line employee in any of these companies shares the same view on the purpose of the business as the Chief Executive Officer does. And *that* is powerful. The most successful organizations in the world have a shared mindset."

Richard Sheridan, CEO of Menlo Innovations, echoed those sentiments on the importance of team performance in a 2016 article in *Inc.* magazine online, and extended them to another more-radical conclusion:

> *Stop doing annual performance reviews. Now. This minute. Send out a message telling everyone on staff that you've banished this tortuous rite from your company.*
>
> *You won't be alone. Microsoft, The Gap, and General Electric have all scrapped the formal year-end rite. Accenture recently announced that it was canning the process. My company, Menlo Innovations, hasn't done a single formal performance review in its 14-year history. It's among the reasons we're so successful.*

> *Annual reviews do more harm than good. If you doubt that, ask yourselves these two questions about your own process:*
>
> - *Does anyone feel better as a result?*
> - *Is there any evidence that the company benefits?*
>
> *In his book,* Out of the Crisis, *quality guru W. Edwards Deming identifies "evaluation of performance, merit rating or annual review" as one of the "seven deadly diseases of management." Deming writes: "The idea of a merit rating is alluring. The sound of the words captivates the imagination: pay for what you get; get what you pay for; motivate people to do their best, for their own good. The effect is exactly the opposite of what the words promise."*
>
> *The chief problem with the annual review is that it pits the performance of the individual against the performance of the team.*

We explained the evil consequences of individual goals in great depth in *Building Engaged Team Performance,* so we won't belabor that point further here. Though this may sound like heresy to some, individuals don't need daily production *goals*; they need to compare their weekly and monthly performance to *standards* in order to get feedback that they can use to improve their performance. Change a culture of blame to a culture of learning. And then the team can just focus every day on the team goal of simply getting all of the work done.

Sadly, the idea of getting rid of productivity goals in general is a "lightning rod" concept that can start arguments with leaders who misunderstand our point. We're not saying that people shouldn't be productive. On the contrary, a key part of building a Lean Culture of Engaged Team Performance is getting the team engaged in performing productively. We're just saying that *productivity goals don't make people productive!*

We'll show you another way.

A NEW WAY OF MEASURING PRODUCTIVITY

In contrast, a better way to think of productivity goals is within the context of standard time, which we discussed back in Step 2 *(Identify Opportunity: Measure and Analyze the Process)*. In that previous chapter, we saw that with an appropriately sized time study of the work, we could get a reliably predictable calculation of the work time needed to do each task. We used that data to right-size the team in Step 5 *(Transform: Organize the Team)*, and then we were able to simply set a team goal of keeping up with the work.

All of these steps and concepts have now come together.

Finally, since the team is now right-sized, the team members will all just need to collaborate and give a full individual effort in order to get all of the work done, because they have barely enough capacity to meet the demand. So now all we need to do is provide feedback to teams and individuals on how much work they're accomplishing compared to the standard time that it should take to do the work. This information is useful for:

- *Leaders:* so they can continually right-size teams for the workload, giving their teams the chance to meet their customers' needs efficiently
- *Teams:* so they can feel confident that all team members are contributing fairly and that the team as a whole is operating efficiently
- *Individuals:* so they can be recognized for their contributions in getting work done

Fortunately, we'll see as we proceed that this feedback drives self-correcting productivity in a right-sized-team that has a team goal of meeting the customers' needs. Once they understand the measurement process, team members are willing to support it because they know that the standard time data came from their own self-reported time study.

As one person explained it, "If the future is that we'll be measured on our performance and required to be efficient as a team, at least I want the team to be measured fairly."

To provide that fair feedback, we use the Efficiency Chart. This is another new tool that you won't yet find in many Lean Culture transformations because it relies on the time study data that many teams haven't yet collected. Conceptually, the Efficiency Chart works by showing *what your team got done* compared to *what your team should have gotten done in the time they had available,* given the standard time to do all of that same work.

Here are the steps to create an Efficiency Chart, which we'll demonstrate with an example:

1. Conduct a time study to determine the *Standard Time Per Task.*
2. Use historical volumes and standard time per task to establish *Work Completion Time Credit.*
3. Gather actual time worked to determine *Available Production Time.*

4. Determine the gap between available production time and work completed to identify *Opportunity for Capacity Change*.

When we introduced the concept of standard time in the Measurement and Analysis phase, we discussed the value of the time study in capturing the average time that it takes to do each type of task, as well as the variation in that work time. We also discussed the idea that while time study data is great for setting standards, we shouldn't use self-reported data directly to manage performance, since it can create a conflict of interest by incenting inaccurate reporting, rewarding those who might provide false information and punishing those who tell the truth.

The Efficiency Chart tool allows us to measure the expectations for productivity in a new way. Here's what the team's Efficiency Chart first looks like when it's deployed. The example in Figure 19 comes from the bank team in 2010, which we introduced in a previous chapter.

Following along by the steps we listed above:

1. Conduct a time study to determine the *Standard Time Per Task*.

   First, we set the standard time for each item of work using the averages that we obtained from the time study. We can also do regression analysis to come up with more accurate drivers of timing, particularly for tasks that have attribute-driven variation.

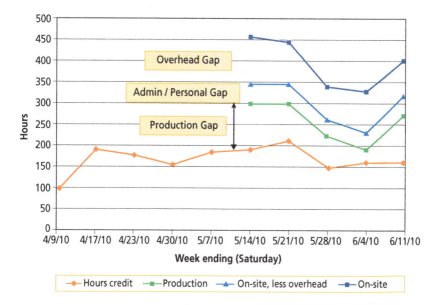

Figure 19 Bank operations team efficiency chart.

2. Use historical volumes and standard time per task to establish *Work Completion Time Credit*.

   Then we count the number of completions of each type of work performed in a certain time period and multiply those counts by the standard time for each work type to calculate the hours of work credit. Since we know the standard times for each task, we don't have to continue to track how long people actually spend on each task; we just need a way of counting who completed what work on what day. Most workflow systems can tell us that, but sometimes we have to create special queries or tracking systems to get that information. This calculation forms the bottom line on the chart in Figure 19.

3. Gather actual time worked to determine *Available Production Time*.

   We then gather the time available to create the top three lines on the chart from time and attendance information from employees, and we ask them to also report non-production overhead (e.g., meetings, training, mentoring, breaks, etc.) so that overhead time can be subtracted from their on-site time to obtain the available production time.

4. Determine the gap between available production time and work completion credit to identify *Opportunity for Capacity Change*.

   Finally, the bottom-up completion credit is compared to the top-down available production time, and we're able to see how much of the available time was converted into work completion. Any gap becomes an opportunity for improvement as a team, depending on the situation:

   – If the team isn't keeping up with potential work volumes, a gap on the chart will show the team an opportunity to get more work done. This is usually not the case.

   – If the team is keeping up with volumes, however, a gap in the chart is an opportunity for leaders to cross-level work from other teams, assign team members to other roles and special projects temporarily, or allow attrition to occur and decline to fill open positions.

The bank team in the example above did their time study prior to this period (in March of 2010) and then implemented the volume tracking, combining their completion count information with the standard times from the time study to calculate the work credit line on the bottom. After gathering the data for a few weeks (each point on the chart is a week), they implemented the top-down tracking in mid-May, which began to provide the top three lines. To get the top-down information, they collected three numbers from each employee each week and then aggregated them for the team:

- *On-site time:* total time worked, which doesn't include paid time off
- *On-site, less overhead:* starts with on-site time, then subtracts training, meetings, and other non-production work from the total time on-site
- *Production time:* subtracts a "personal time assumption" of 1 hour per 8-hour day from the "on-site, less overhead" time to derive the time available for production work

For this particular team, the organization had streamlined some processes, including the account closure payments that we discussed in a prior chapter, but they had not yet done a right-sizing reorganization, and so they had a Production gap: there was a substantial gap between the Production time and the Work Credit lines (the bottom two lines). With 11 people on the team, the Production gap of about 75 hours per week, about 2 FTE, seemed rather unbelievable.

So we watched the data for a few more weeks and started to find other work and special projects for team members to do. Figure 20 shows the same team with three more months of data.

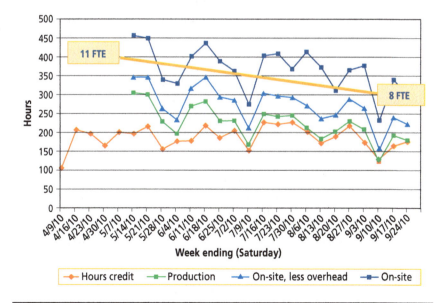

Figure 20 Bank operations team efficiency improvement.

It turns out the gap was three FTE. It took the leadership team about four weeks to gain confidence that the gap was real and that the team had more capacity to get more work done. The key moment occurred on the week ending July 9, when the team realized that they could get 150 hours' worth of work done and still make time for their 4th of July Weekend festivities.

Holidays are good for testing productivity because they reduce capacity when people take time off, while the team often needs to meet close-to-normal work demand. On that holiday week, the teams saw that the available Production time and the work Credit time were very close to equal. When everyone saw that, they started to believe that the charts were telling the truth.

Once leaders were completely convinced, we started sharing the team chart with all of the team members, and we reminded them that we'd be starting to produce individual charts the next month to allow team leaders to give each person efficiency feedback. As you can see from the chart, the productivity gap quickly started to tighten.

The leadership team knew they couldn't just ask the team to work harder, though. As we've said over and over, individual efficiency wasn't the problem. There was extra capacity on the team, but there was also a clear and stable history of the work credit (the bottom line on the chart) that averaged 175 hours per week. The main problem was that there wasn't enough work to do to support a team of that size.

That problem came to our attention in a very personal way, as everyone started to realize that the team was a bit overstaffed. I was in the cafeteria at lunchtime, and one of the employees sat down at my table, tears streaming down her cheeks. She explained that she had seen the team efficiency chart and wanted to know which people we were intending to fire. She said she really needed her job and would try to work harder. She didn't understand (or perhaps, didn't yet believe) the longer-term vision that we had for right-sizing the team slowly over time through attrition as people moved to new roles. Nobody needed to lose his or her job.

So the leadership team candidly communicated the vision for right-sizing, and they started finding special projects for the meantime, siphoning off a few people to work on other things until they had enough attrition to slowly reduce the team size over a number of months. By the end of September, there were eight engaged team members doing the work that the team of eleven had been doing in March.

Nobody left involuntarily, and the eight remaining team members had much safer jobs. The employee who had been so worried still works there, and she's completely engaged and positive about the team's work and her role in it.

STEALING WORK

The concept of having enough work to do is pretty important. As we've said, a team with too little work can't be efficient. We like to compare an underfed production team to a racehorse waking around the track, developing bad habits because it can't get a proper workout. You might think that team members would enjoy a light workload. Counterintuitively, it's no fun to be on an over-capacity team because the team members are constantly worried that someone will realize that they're not busy enough and cut their jobs, and there's really nothing they can do about it. They feel the axe hanging over their heads.

Once we were called in to lead a short project with an existing client. When we asked what their objectives were, the leader said, "People are stealing work from each other."

"Say, what?" I asked. That was my first time hearing that one. An anti-collaborative norm?

"Our team does telephone application calls to underwrite life insurance policies. Each day we get a list of appointments to call, with pre-set times arranged to call each proposed insured person, and then we call them and spend about 20 minutes on the phone with each one. Each team member is assigned to do one call every half-hour, but recently we've been hearing some employees say that by the time they attempt their calls, there's no appointment left in the queue. Another team member must have taken two during that 30-minute block."

You won't be shocked to find out that the leadership team had recently instituted a count-based individual goal *(uh-oh!)* for each person to complete a certain number of calls per day.

Knowing that it wasn't possible to complete two calls in the time that the appointments were supposed to take, we quickly learned from team members that the behavior was being caused by a "no-show" on the client's part. When a team member called a client and didn't get an answer, they knew that they would not meet their goals for the day, and so some of them were moving on to the next call on the list, which of course "belonged" to someone else. After measuring the no-shows for a few weeks, we found that they were happening at a very predictable rate of 30%. The individual goals were causing the problem, and the team was inefficient not because of bad work habits but because there wasn't enough work to do.

As you may guess, we just implemented two changes: (1) overbooked the calls by 30% based on the historical data, and (2) changed to a team goal of getting all the work done. We got more work done without anyone having to steal it.

CHANGING NEGATIVE CULTURE TO POSITIVE

When you deploy team efficiency charts in concert with whiteboards and team goals of getting all of the work done, the feedback becomes self-correcting, which works much better than pushing individuals with count-based performance goals.

To illustrate the difference, think of the classic situation of each person being accountable for delivering a certain number of units per day of work. Have you ever seen these behaviors?

- *Cherry-picking:* individuals spend time looking through the worklist to find the easier items to complete when they need quick credit
- *Saving completions:* when individuals get ahead on work for the day, they can save completions for the following day (sales people do this with their quarterly goals too)
- *Pacing:* when the reward for early completion of "my work" is just to help someone else with "their work," people pace themselves to finish it just on time before the due date
- *Negative peer pressure:* an individual who does more than the minimum goal will be "taken behind the woodshed" by other employees and told to slow down
- *Negative feelings:* individual goals can fail to motivate people because they quite-rightly realize that the goals are just intended to make them work harder

All of those are very real, negative consequences of individual goals. By using the standard time in a different way, however, we are able to give differential credit for work items with different levels of complexity. Rather than looking at this information for each individual on a daily basis to bludgeon people for poor performance, we prefer to use the team data to drive a positive environment of collaboration with accountability to meet the customers' needs. There are a number of reasons that the team data view is more useful:

- *Cherry-credit:* longer tasks get more time credit than shorter ones, removing any advantage that would come from cherry-picking the easier work
- *Variation:* an individual might truthfully say that one particular item took "longer than usual" today, and so daily performance at an individual level has too much variation in it, while daily team performance has a large enough sample size to overcome that variation; weekly or monthly data, however, turns out to be very accurate at an individual view and is useful and fair for performance management discussions

- *Positive peer pressure:* when the team goal is just to "get all of the work done," the peer pressure changes from negative ("slow down so you don't embarrass everyone else") to positive ("speed up so we can all go home when the work is done")
- *Line of sight to the customer:* team members feel much better about their goals when they can feel the connection between the goal and their customers' needs

The bottom line here is that the Efficiency Chart is a new and very powerful tool to support the most important team goal we've set for "getting all the work done today" in Step 6, *Engage! Set Team Goals.* Team goals and Efficiency Charts nicely and positively reinforce the important accountabilities of living in a Lean Culture by being a contributing member of an Engaged Team.

LEADING TEAM GOAL-SETTING

I read an article recently that bothered me. I had to remember what my wife Celeste sometimes says, perhaps just to encourage me in my own writing endeavors, that "you don't have to be right to write a book." She usually continues with something really supportive like, "A lot of idiots have gotten published…"

Anyway, the article was entitled something like "Why Measuring Efficiency is Anti-Lean" and the premise was that efficiency measures are bad. I strongly disagree. Efficiency measures are only bad in the hands of unenlightened leaders. Efficiency measures don't unfairly judge people; bad leaders unfairly judge people!

Team goals that relate to real customer needs will make sense to team members, and right-sized teams can certainly be expected to keep up with their workload and work efficiently in order to meet those customers' needs. Efficiency measures help leaders and teams know what those expectations should be.

So as you lead the development of your team goals, consider:

1. What do your customers really need, and how can you set team goals that directly support delivering excellent service to customers? Can you get past the "minimum requirement" and get teams to buy in to concepts such as Mission Zero that deliver optimum value for both you and your customers?
2. Do you have measures in place so that you know how you're performing, and are those performance data available in real time? How do you need to resource the necessary reporting functions?

3. How can you convince leaders to use efficiency data for the right things (right-sizing their teams, making good decisions to add or re-hire open positions) instead of the wrong things (pushing people to "stretch" or punishing the lower end of the performance curve)?

A right-sized team (from Step 5), supported by streamlined processes (from Step 3) and visual data (from Step 4), just needs a team goal and an Efficiency Chart to guide it (in Step 6). As we've said before, we teach and discuss those concepts one at a time, but you really may need to implement a combination of them all at once, depending on your situation. Regardless, all of that change management takes great leadership to implement, which we'll discuss in Step 7, *Implement Change: Lead the Transition*.

And then as we'll see in Step 8, the leader can get out of the way and let the team manage itself, while shifting focus to strategy, employee development, innovation, and sustaining the Lean Culture.

7

Implement Change: Lead the Transition

L'audace, l'audace, toujours l'audace.
Audacity, audacity. Always audacity.

Danton, and later, General George S. Patton

The toughest part of a Lean Culture transformation often comes when people start to see the potential changes that are coming and begin to think about the impact more personally. While the change resistance that naturally develops can sometimes make the transformation feel like an uphill battle, the leader's role is to reverse that feeling and make it a downhill battle.

THE UPHILL BATTLE

Hardly anyone disagrees with the transformation approach when we're envisioning perfection or mapping the current state processes at the beginning of the effort, and while it's sometimes a bit of a pain, time study data collection during the measurement phase generally doesn't become a change management nightmare either. Transformation teams, business leaders, and departmental team members are often curious about the ultimate direction of the effort, and they're willing to reserve judgment and play along at the beginning.

But once we get into the later phases, when the team starts to come up with new ideas to change processes, organizational design, job roles, team goals, and individual performance accountabilities, some passive resistance and/or active disagreement will eventually come out.

While we won't repeat the cycle of change acceptance theory from *Building Engaged Team Performance*, we'll suffice it to say that the resistance comes from anyone and everyone, and most of them (even leaders) are worried about how the potential changes will impact them personally. For the most part, transformation leaders can get through this phase by layering the scary ideas in over time, but sometimes the resistance comes to a head during this part of the deployment.

The truth is that change is inevitable, and becoming good at leading change is the only real source of long-term competitive advantage. Yet it's still scary and some people still resist.

Sometimes it feels like an uphill battle for the transformation's leadership, getting everyone to try to pilot the change concepts so that they can experience how the future will be better, while allowing the team to come to grips with the reality that everything will be okay for them personally. Roles may change; the process may change; the organization may look different. But progress marches on, and you can either march with it or get stepped on.

Speaking of marching, that reminds me of a story...

A DOWNHILL BATTLE

In early July of 1863, the Confederate Army (with red arrows on the map that follows) made its way toward a small Pennsylvania town called Gettysburg, and the Union Army set up defensive positions along the high ground between Cemetery Ridge and a couple of hills called Round Top. As the Confederates advanced to seize that high ground on the left flank of the Union line, a regiment called the 20th Maine, led by Colonel Joshua L. Chamberlain, took hasty positions near the top of the smaller hill. Fittingly, that hill's name was Little Round Top. See Figure 21.

As the Confederates attacked the hill throughout the day on July 2, Chamberlain and his team understood the criticality of their position on the flank, where the enemy could roll up the entire Union line on Cemetery Ridge to the north if the 20th's position were to fall. They fought hard, repelling two major attacks.

And then they ran out of ammunition.

Chamberlain could hear the Confederate unit below him on the hill, preparing for one final attack. He didn't have time to retreat, and he knew that staying in position would result in being overrun. He was left with no other choice, and so he quickly made a decision that changed the outcome of the battle and most likely the war.

"Fix bayonets. Charge!"

Without ammunition, the 20th Maine used the only weapons they had: the bayonets attached to the ends of their guns. As Chamberlain and his men attacked down the hill, the Confederate units thought they were faced with a superior-sized force and they fled.

It was a downhill battle for Chamberlain and his team because they had no other choice, but Chamberlain had the audacity and presence of mind to order the improbable attack. His soldiers followed him down the hill that day, loyal from the trust his leadership had built in them over time. And so together they won the battle and turned the tide of the war.

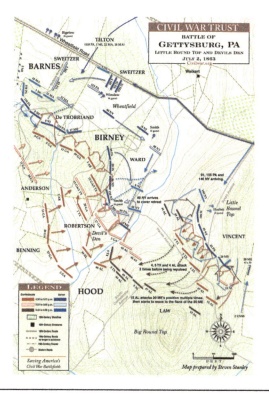

Figure 21 The Battle of Gettysburg.
(http://www.civilwar.org/battlefields/gettysburg/maps/gettysburg-devils-den-and.html).

Chamberlain was wounded six times in his service during the American Civil War, and he ended up in Appomattox at the end, ceremoniously accepting the Confederate Army's surrender. His Medal of Honor citation from the action at Gettysburg reads:

> *The President of the United States of America, in the name of Congress, takes pleasure in presenting the Medal of Honor to Colonel Joshua Lawrence Chamberlain, United States Army, for extraordinary heroism on 2 July 1863, while serving with 20th Maine Infantry, in action at Gettysburg, Pennsylvania, for daring heroism and great tenacity in holding his position on the Little Round Top against repeated assaults, and carrying the advance position on the Great Round Top.*

He was in the right place at the right time and made the right decision, mostly because he didn't have any other choice. But if Chamberlain hadn't been such a great leader, perhaps his soldiers wouldn't have followed him down the hill that day. Leadership matters.

REBELLION OR REVOLUTION?

There comes a time in every change effort when the team has to decide whether to forge ahead or retreat. We might call that the "rebellion" phase of the transformation.

Every transformation effort, and we mean *every one*, faces a rebellion at some point.

Usually it comes in the later steps, once the team has studied the process, collected some data, and begun to discuss some general concepts for change. As we've said, while studying processes and collecting data can sometimes feel painful, it's hard to argue against those activities. Who can admit to being against measuring processes and performance?

But unfortunately, it's all too easy to be against a specific solution, so once a few of those are on the table, the resistance to change can start to tumble out. And that's usually the critical moment in the transformation effort.

In a recent project, a team discussed a new concept that might or might not have been a good idea, but they recommended a pilot to try it out to see if and how it might work. One leader was worried about the implications and took the issue to a more senior leader, who decided to defer the proposed pilot to focus on developing more-tactical ideas first. Unfortunately, that decision sent a message to the organization that the scarier changes could be successfully thwarted, and the team's commitment to conceiving big ideas quickly ebbed away. The organization got some things implemented, but they missed considering some of the more radical and possibly more impactful solutions. They changed some processes, but they didn't change the organization or its culture.

The really funny thing about the story above? Some teams are reading this right now and saying, "Yeah, that was us." You're not alone.

So, regardless of where the resistance initially comes from and how well founded it is in fact, the first rebellion becomes a test of fortitude. Often mid-level and senior leaders are left to decide whether to move forward or to err on the side of caution. In these situations, we usually ask a simple question:

If we can figure out a fairly risk-free way to pilot the new concept, what's the harm in trying it?

Rich Sheridan echoes that thought in *Joy, Inc.,* encouraging rapid experimentation to learn from mistakes instead of living in fear of making them:

> *In order to try anything really new, you should start small. Small gives you space to run cheap experiments that barely register if they don't work out. If a "make mistakes faster" culture is going to survive and thrive, you must establish a standard of fast, frequent, and inexpensive experimentation.*

REVOLUTION

Piloting new ideas is the way to get past the rebellion and move on to the revolution. The ideas sink or swim on their own merit, and the act of trying something new energizes the team. Ideas that had seemed impossible soon evolve into solid solutions, which quickly get implemented and yield amazing results.

Do you know the difference between a rebellion and a revolution? History is the judge. If you fight and lose, they call it a rebellion; if you fight and win, it's a revolution.

To paraphrase a famous Beatles song, we say we want a revolution. We want to change the process, the organization, and the team's performance in a profound way. We all want to change the world.

CIRCLES AND TRIANGLES

At the point where it's time to change, a leader has to lead; whether on a battlefield or in implementing a new Lean Culture of Engaged Team Performance, leadership matters. And so as we've introduced the concepts of engaged teams, we haven't yet thrown our support fully behind the new age concepts of *leaderless* teams, for example the "Holacracy" practiced at Zappos.com and some other companies. Those are audacious experiments in human behavior, and they haven't yet stood the test of time. But they have great intentions and promise.

Zappos.com's version of Holacracy creates circles of roles, replacing the business hierarchy triangles of layered leadership with a flatter organization. Each circle has a "lead" role that facilitates the self-directed work team, but the person isn't a "supervisor" in the traditional sense of that function in other companies. It's an interesting experiment, and it seems to be working for them.

Ironically though, even in the story of Zappos' deployment of their new management system, their CEO had to aggressively lead the changes that got rid of the classic management hierarchy. So as we proceed, we'll illustrate that even the greatest proponents of self-directed teams had to exert great leadership in their organizations to make the transition.

LEADING ENGAGEMENT IN CHANGE

As we have demonstrated in stories in previous chapters, employee involvement in the other six phases leading up to that transformation is one of the keys to gaining change acceptance during the transition to a Lean Culture. By assigning a transformation team with a mixture of leaders and front-line production employees to lead the organization through the steps, we not only get better solutions, but we also get much greater acceptance across the organization. Similarly, people can support the idea of using the results of the time study for setting standards for performance because everyone participated in the time study to provide that data.

And then as we mentioned in Step 5, *Transform: Organize the Team,* the best way to gain support for the new Lean Culture is to have a team try it out. By experimenting with organizational transformations, process improvement solutions, and visual data controls on a pilot team or two, the whole organization can see and feel the power of the Lean Culture and get excited about their turn to implement it.

Zappos.com took a similar path to their transformation. They planned it meticulously and tried it for a while.

But in early 2015, after piloting their new Holacracy management approach for two years, Zappos' CEO Tony Hsieh abruptly accelerated his implementation plan by sending a long email to his company and telling everyone to get on board or take a severance package.

Now.

According to *Business Insider,* "When Hsieh sent the memo in March [2015], 85% of the company had already begun the transition to Holacracy, but the urgency in the email and the weight of the offer shocked even the most loyal Zapponian." An astounding 18% of the company ended up leaving, but those who remained were fully committed to the approach.

As Rich Sheridan says in *Joy, Inc.*, "Leading cultural change is a very lonely pursuit."

When the team needs to overcome resistance to change, the leadership team has to find a way to make it clear to the team members that there is no option to retreat. It's a downhill battle. To paraphrase the Oracle in *The Matrix,* find a way to convince everyone that, "You've already made your choice. Now you just have to understand it."

Chamberlain's 20th Maine didn't have another option. Tony Hsieh's Zappos employees exercised their options and the company was left with those who wanted to stay. Regardless, find a way to make your uphill battle into a downhill battle.

Here are some questions you can ask:

1. How can you get everyone to pilot or try the new ideas? If you've given enough authority to your Lean transformation team, you may be able to just let them take the lead and ride the transformation process through to its inevitable conclusion, but watch out for mid-level leaders who may try to derail it. Whom do you need to influence to get on board?

2. If you do encounter some resistance, should you wait for critical mass of acceptance to develop, or should you mandate an action like Chamberlain and Hsieh did? You'll have to read the situation. If you encounter serious resistance, it's most likely to come from a leader in your organization who just doesn't want to change. To paraphrase Thomas Jefferson, sometimes the tree of engagement needs to be refreshed with the blood of resisters. And to paraphrase George S. Patton, when that time comes, you'll know what you have to do.

3. When the right time arrives to commit, how can you "burn the lifeboats" or make it a downhill battle so that there's no option to go back?

There will come a time when you have to lead people down that hill, because leadership matters and that's what leaders do. Be ready when the time comes.

Fix bayonets. Charge.

8

Stand the Test of Time: Sustain Lean Engaged Team Performance

You've probably seen or heard for yourself of some great results from Lean efforts that weren't sustained over time. As we discussed in the first chapter, the vast majority of organizations claim to have experienced the same challenge.

Even some of the process streamlining stories we discussed in previous chapters of this book have failed to sustain their results through the publishing date. It's certainly not all of them, but are you really surprised?

PROCESS-ONLY FOCUS LEADS TO FAILURE

At the beginning of this book, we shared data from a survey that claimed that only two percent of Lean Deployments meet their organizations' goals, and we said that the cause was often an imbalance between focus on process streamlining for waste reduction (a great thing) and the intent to create a sustainable Lean Culture (a much greater thing). Another real-life testimony to that paradox comes from a friend I mentioned in an earlier chapter, though we'll still protect the identity of her organization for some obvious reasons:

> We had a new leader come into the company, said we were going to do Lean Six Sigma, delegated the implementation, then left about half a year later. An initial green belt training was held. The Six Sigma data analysis was pretty challenging, so the person responsible for implementation decided to focus on Lean for removing waste and brought in another vendor to deliver Lean training. When the leader who had mandated Lean Six Sigma left, the remaining leadership team said Lean seems like a good idea, keep doing it.

> But it was a rubber stamp approval: "You go do that, and let us know how it's going." They didn't know what support was needed from them to make it successful. They had approved it and funded it.
>
> Training was elective, and people would sign up for training because they were interested and get all excited about the opportunities they saw for Lean. Then they would go back to their daily work and either not be able to get Lean projects started, or start them and run into a roadblock and abandon them. Lean was not seen as the way of doing business, but as another idea of the month that would go away.
>
> When pitched with an idea for a Lean improvement, leaders would rubber stamp it, pay no attention to the outcomes, and allow firefighting and production peaks to derail the Lean efforts. Lean projects were not seen as a priority, so people didn't want to dedicate the time. We would work in two- to four-hour chunks, spread over months. Either the current state had changed by the time we got to future state, or the future state was never implemented, or by the time we had completed current state there was a new priority and the Lean work was set aside.
>
> A new leader, who had previously worked for a company that did Lean, came in and asked for someone on the leadership team to volunteer to run three projects in their area over the next fiscal year with dedicated resources to do week-long kaizen events and implementation. Then he would come back to the leadership team to demonstrate the results. Within the first year, those projects were yielding six-figure results.

Leadership matters.

CULTURE CRASH

A long-running success recently headed south, and you can guess why: leadership. The team had improved performance steadily, with multiple waves of Lean transformation efforts spread over almost a decade, and they were among the best of their industry benchmarks for high speed, great service, and low cost. Improvement, engagement, and excellence had become embedded in their culture. They had strong senior leadership in place. And then they got hit by a perfect storm of leadership challenges:

- Their senior operations director retired. While a few folks joked that "nobody really knew what he did all day anyway" and pretended not to miss him, they soon realized that he was the glue that held all of the parts of the organization together. He believed in visible metrics and management by walking around. He was always present in his team's work areas. Sometimes the best leaders are the quiet ones who don't get much attention.
- At the same time, their senior operations manager, who reported to the retiring director, was given a promotion and a new department assignment. He deserved that new opportunity because of the changes he had led and the culture he had developed in the department over the last half-decade, but it hurt deeply to lose two levels of strong leadership at the same time.
- A new leader came in from another place in the company, immediately making her mark by challenging the metrics that were shared daily. "The whiteboard takes too long to prepare every day," she said, distracting team members from actually getting work done. She told the executive team that she was suspending the data monitoring and visual controls for a while so that they could reassess their effectiveness.

Whoosh. It was as though a hurricane had hit the place and sucked the culture right out of the building.

There were a couple key questions that the executives didn't get a chance to ask (or perhaps didn't get the right answer to...), such as:

1. *Why did the whiteboard now take too long to update every day?* It turned out that the whiteboard was easy to update when the work was under control, but counting the available work took too long when the team was backlogged. And the team had gotten backlogged right when the new leader assumed control. The problem wasn't the time it took to count the work; the problem was the increase in backlog of work itself.

2. *Why was the team backlogged?* There were a few reasons: (a) the new leader believed that delivering work before it was "due" was inefficient, so she had told her teams to stop over-servicing the customers and work on other projects instead of getting work done quickly; (b) there had been some quality issues recently, so the new leader suggested that people "slow down and do it right" even though the data showed that the quality issues weren't correlated with speed (defects weren't predominately coming from "faster" people); and (c) once the whiteboards were

discontinued, the backlog problem was out of sight and out of mind and the work queues grew quietly until it was too late. At that point, the backlog began to generate additional work (status calls, prioritization, etc.), but the team was no longer sized with the capacity to spend additional time on those non-value-added tasks; they had to start scrambling and working overtime to get all the work done. The snowball of work became an avalanche.

It was a classic crash in the process, caused by new leaders making decisions that they didn't fully understand. Years of culture-building were razed to the ground in a few months.

The root cause of that leadership problem was that the department was an "island of Lean Culture" within a larger company that didn't yet quite get it. So when a few key leaders left the team, the leaders who replaced them didn't know how to sustain the culture.

The solution to this is very simple: all leaders in the organization, starting at the top, have to first understand and then commit to implementing and sustaining the principles of Lean Engaged Team Performance. Contrary to what Jack Welch said in the conference story of a previous chapter, though, if you are trying to transform your department on your own and the senior leadership team members above you aren't driving that culture too, first consider trying to change the world one piece at a time. Make a difference where you are. Set a great example and show other leaders around you how you did it. Teach them and encourage them. Be a voice for change. Try to work upstream and expand the Lean Culture throughout your company, because your pocket of excellence may not stand the test of time unless you surround it with others.

Unfortunately, all of that is very easy to say and very hard to do. The necessary Lean Culture leadership skills don't come from the ubiquitous two-day sheep-dip Executive Green Belt class. That kind of training sets your team on the right path, but the experiences that leaders need can only come from developing positive habits over time through a deeper deployment strategy. They have to learn by winning.

RESOURCING A SUSTAINABLE TRANSFORMATION

In the end, it will take a committed and knowledgeable C-level leader, usually a CEO directly sponsoring the effort. Sometimes a COO, CFO, or CIO can champion the effort from the Operations, Finance, or Information Technology divisions if she or he can set the agenda for the entire leadership team. While we've seen successful transformations led from Strategy or Human Resources departments, it doesn't send exactly the same message to the organization as someone leading it from the C level. If you don't have that person at the top on board yet, run a pilot in an area that you do control, and then show everyone the results. Work your way up the organization by winning.

Regardless, a leader has to set a vision for a Lean Culture of Engaged Team Performance and then resource the transformation with key infrastructure investments, which we'll detail below.

Training:

First, while we've argued against relying on "sheep-dip training" to deliver culture change, it's certainly a key component in getting started. Most deployments include training for everyone in Lean Engaged Team Performance principles with supporting coaching, including:

- Kaizen and 5S for all employees and leaders
- Lean Transformation principles and metrics for all leaders
- Lean Engaged Team Performance project management for facilitators

The critical difference, however, is that you have to follow the training with other investments in resources, time, leadership involvement, empowerment, and communication.

Resources:

You'll need to establish dedicated roles for certifying and sustaining the infrastructure of people, process, and technology, including:

- Project managers and facilitators with experience in Lean transformation, Kaizen, 5S, Six Sigma, Agile, and standard project management techniques
- Data analysts to maintain trend charts, efficiency charts, quality controls, and other key performance data
- Business analysts to document the business process architecture and related systems

Time:

The most critical investment is the time needed to spend on process and performance improvement (e.g., Kaizen and 5S), at all levels of the organization. After the initial launch, which will require a temporary investment of additional resources, some of that time may be created or freed up from initial process improvement efforts if some of the gains are rolled back into the transformation instead of fully "cashed in" (e.g., by reducing staff).

Eventually, the organization has to be resourced for sustainability. Improving processes, transforming organizations, and sustaining culture takes time and work, and while it may take more effort at the beginning, you'll have to sustain some level of effort forever in order to continue to grow and improve.

Leader Involvement:

My friend who lived through a Lean deployment championed by "hands-off" leadership expands on the criticality of senior leaders being involved:

> *I think this part is the day-to-day stuff that leaders get too busy to do; then they get out of touch and make disconnected decisions. Leaders have to take the time themselves to go to training, be at improvement events and report-outs, be visible, stay in touch during implementation, and make sure the team knows they are paying attention. They also have to make the training and time for improvement and gathering the metrics a priority for their teams. Stay in touch and remove barriers to participation.*

Empowerment:

As we've discussed in previous chapters, senior leaders have to transfer authority to enable the cross-functional and cross-level transformation team(s) to try new things. Employees and leaders who participate in Kaizen events, 5S, and larger departmental transformations have to feel empowered to pilot new solutions. Leaders must agree to key groundrules and be willing to let the teams pilot *anything* that might allow the organization to learn something new, even if they don't themselves think that it will work.

Communication:

Leaders have to continually communicate the vision, purpose, and direction for the Lean Culture transformation. Even if you start to think you're repeating yourself, it's possible that you're communicating barely enough!

By using "band and brand" analogies in his book, *Culture That Rocks*, Jim Knight emphasizes the importance of communication in developing a shared culture:

> *Considered one of the biggest bands on the planet, U2 consists of four members, yet many people do not know the names of the bass guitarist or the drummer. Adam Clayton and Larry Mullen Jr. — the lesser-known musicians in the band — make up the group's critical rhythm section. They certainly don't get the notoriety of the band's other two members, but they are perfectly cool with their roles.*

Additionally, Adam and Larry have claimed in interviews that each time they play to a packed arena on tour, they are trying to duplicate exactly what they did the night before. The same show, night after night driven by consistency. They're the steady engines driving the band.

Yet, if you listen to discussions with Bono or The Edge—the more well-known, public faces of U2—these two rock stars admit they are trying to do something completely different from the night before. They're trying to soar the band to new heights and create something uniquely spectacular with each performance.

With the combination of these two different approaches to performing, all four members of U2 understand both their individual roles and the collective mindset that makes this band one of history's rock treasures. Group members are all on the same page and understand their independent responsibilities while also supporting the ultimate goal of the band: to make some of the greatest music of all time.

What's true for a rock group is also true when it comes to an organization and its makeup. It doesn't matter if you're the brand-new technician at the auto repair shop, the dishwasher at the restaurant, the administrative assistant at a technology giant or the toll attendant on a major highway... everybody has a part to play in the band. Maybe the lead singer or front guy will always get the glory, but every person in a high-performing organization knows that he or she has a crucial part to play in the band's success.

This keen awareness—when all team members understand the company's mission, their specific, individual roles, and how the company stacks up against the competition—doesn't happen by accident. It occurs when the organization's leadership makes a clear choice to keep the employees as "in the loop" as possible about all things related to their jobs and the brand. That is, those at the top make a conscious decision to over-communicate to employees and ensure they are informed, aware, and involved with the inner-workings of the organization and its culture. Individuals may take different paths to create a result, but if the overall result is on par with your mission statement and based on shared mindsets, phenomenal success will be within reach. Abundant and transparent communication ensures that all team members are singing off the same sheet of music.

U2's culture rocks. Yours can too.

EXPANDING THE LEAN CULTURE

After dedicating the necessary infrastructure, you have to transform your company one department at a time. Think globally but act locally. Culture change happens on the work floor with each departmental team.

Jana Schmidt initially launched the transformation effort at Ecova by tasking David Cline with leading their business process improvement (BPI) efforts in her Sales and Operations group, starting with piloting grass-roots projects throughout the organization. As those efforts began to garner attention and deliver results, the BPI team expanded the effort across the organization by doing brief assessments in each department and feeding those leaders who were most interested with the resources to facilitate their transformations. Positive results drove positive peer pressure to engage at the leader level, and eventually almost everyone in one of the main business units had gone through the transformation steps.

Cline remembers, "A different atmosphere was occurring in our operational units with the result of collaboration being positive energy. Team members became engaged in daily planning and decision making. Once the vision of team success was defined, people began to embrace the culture and people were having fun."

Their culture was heading the right way, and the business results from Lean Engaged Team Performance were quickly becoming significant enough to get noticed. The pilot transformation leaders were presenting their results, both inside and outside the company. Team members were doing huddles around their whiteboards every day and watching their daily visual measures. Anyone walking by could see that something different was happening there. The building blocks were in place.

But while the Lean Culture of Engaged Team Performance was growing throughout the company, it was still growing in the grass-roots. The leadership team hadn't yet incorporated the principles of what Lean calls "Leader Standard Work" from their daily management processes all the way up through their annual planning cycle. The culture had developed, but it hadn't yet been standardized in a way that it could be sustained.

STRATEGY DEPLOYMENT AND LEADER STANDARD WORK

In late 2014, Jana Schmidt's promotion to CEO gave Ecova another chance to change.

Schmidt knew she had to engage her entire leadership team in meeting some audacious goals for 2015, both to find the right opportunities and to execute on them together. She scheduled a set of meetings to engage her entire leadership team in a component of leader standard work that we call strategy deployment.

One often-mentioned critical element of a Lean transformation is development of leader standard work—the daily, weekly, monthly, quarterly, and annual activities that leaders must regularly repeat in order to create a rhythm of continuity in sustaining their teams' performance. Funny enough, everyone agrees that leaders need standard work, but most leaders struggle to figure out what work should be on that list. In addition to the daily activities of walking the work-floor, talking to team members, listening to team huddles, and reviewing visual metrics, leaders need to use data to keep their teams right-sized and focused on improvement through resourcing change initiatives. They need to empower their teams to manage the daily work, so that they can spend their own time on longer-term investments such as recruiting and hiring talent, developing people, and sponsoring improvement projects.

Also known in Lean circles as Hoshin Planning, strategy deployment is another longer-term element of leader standard work that aligns transformation efforts with business priorities, integrating annual and quarterly business planning activities with the Lean transformation to pull the accountability for leaders to spearhead their Lean Engaged Team Performance efforts and sustain them with the right metrics. The word "deployment" is most meaningful; we find that many organizations have a strategy-execution gap between their strategy and their tactics, and so the strategy deployment effort starts with an overview of the business strategy and then derives the right initiatives, priorities, and resource plans to execute that strategy.

In their first strategy deployment workshop, Schmidt's leadership team set goals and agreed upon the overall approach and decision criteria. The next two workshops identified and prioritized all ongoing, proposed, and new potential initiatives that required any type of cross-functional resources. There were dozens of projects on the list. The last workshop set priorities for the upcoming year, cancelling some ongoing efforts, selecting some new initiatives, and clearly prioritizing the resources, scope, and objectives for each effort.

In general, the strategy deployment effort progresses from a general assessment, initially creating an unconstrained list of every possible initiative, creating a description summary of each one, and then applying priorities, timelines, and resource plans to decide upon the right initiatives to launch and/or continue. That approach typically looks like Figure 22.

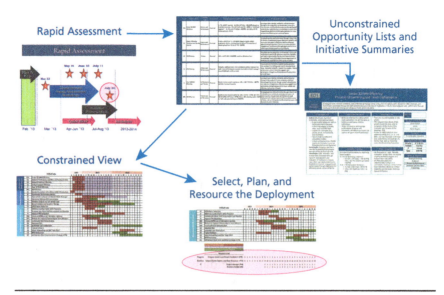

Figure 22 General approach to strategy deployment.

The timeline at Ecova was aggressive, as shown in Figure 23.

Figure 23 Strategy deployment planning at Ecova.

1. Nov. 5 – Launch Workshop (5 hours) – Objectives; opportunities; near-term actions
2. Nov. 19 – Opportunity Workshop (1 day) – Financial commitments; full opportunity list
3. Nov. 24-26 – Annual Operating Plan Reviews – Commitments made
4. Dec. 4 – Solution Structuring Summit (1 day) – What do we do, why, & how… together
5. Dec. 17 – Tactical Project Prioritization (1 day) – Priorities, resources, and project plans

Schmidt explains:

> *It was very empowering to get the key leaders together to talk about what our objectives were and what would be the most meaningful ways we could tackle our goals together. Not only did we have alignment around what we were solving, but we also had full visibility into what we were committing to do as an organization, so that we could better assess our capacity and ability to deliver. Once we agreed on the key projects that would deliver the greatest value, we embraced the same approach to evaluate, design, execute and measure our results. It achieved predictable success and the teams learned repeatable ways to approach business process improvement within their own areas on an ongoing basis.*

SUSTAINING STRATEGY DEPLOYMENT

2015 started fast for Ecova, with new projects of many types launching out of the all-leader strategy deployment efforts. It was a year for execution. Everyone was heads-down working hard on their assigned efforts. At the same time, a number of leaders changed positions, which as we've already discussed can sometimes be the catalyst for either positive change or disaster.

One of the keys to strategy deployment is making it a regular process instead of just an annual event. Schmidt delegated that task to her Chief Business Performance Officer, Lauren Kirkley, who created a solid new process for submitting new efforts for consideration, complete with scoring criteria, charter forms, and monthly strategy deployment and project review meetings.

The team came together to get it done and achieved their financial plan. Schmidt recalls how this experience has shifted her own approach in leading the company toward a positive culture of results:

> *I learned the importance of leadership in managing operational performance tightly with strong leading service indicators that measure the health of the operation. I also saw that, as a leader, I needed to be much more clear to empower and hold accountable my leaders for successful, repeatable, consistent delivery for our clients.*

LEADING AND SUSTAINING LEAN CULTURE

David Marquet says, "Don't empower, emancipate." Whether in engaging teams in work or treating all people with dignity and respect, emancipation is a worthy endeavor. While empowerment is given, sometimes just temporarily, from the leader to the led, emancipation is permanent. He explains:

> *With emancipation, we are recognizing the inherent genius, energy, and creativity in all people, and allowing those talents to emerge. We realize that we don't have the power to give those talents to others, or "empower" them to use them, only the power to prevent them from coming out. Emancipation results when teams have been given decision-making control and have the additional characteristics of competence and clarity. You know you have an emancipated team when you no longer need to empower them. Indeed, you no longer have the ability to empower them because they are not relying on you as their source of power.*

A coach told me once, "You're either getting better or you're getting worse. You can't ever stay the same," so here are some questions for you to consider as you proceed:

1. Are you creating a Culture of Leadership and Learning? Put the books *Turn the Ship Around!* and *Mindset* on your list to read next, and think about how to free your teams from the chains of fixed-mindset thinking and top-down leadership empowerment.

2. Do you have some leaders who can't make the shift to leading in a new Lean Culture? How can you help them change?
3. How will you make sure your Lean Culture survives when you eventually retire or leave the organization?

Sustaining a Lean Culture of Engaged Team Performance is a constant battle. Even the best cultures have their ups and downs.

Lean Culture is a journey, not a destination.

9
Conclusion: New Lean Tools and a New Lean Culture

In this book, we've covered some of the key concepts of Lean, but if you were already familiar with Lean tools and principles, you've probably noted that we didn't attempt to provide a full description of every tool. We focused on a few Lean tools, and we discussed new ways to integrate traditional Lean tools in order to transform organizations and sustain Lean culture better. We've finished every chapter, though, with a focus on leadership.

The main point we've made is that developing a Lean Culture must be an intentional journey that leaders must lead. Leadership must commit to that intention and then must purposefully engage everyone in the transformation. Engagement in a culture is a product of engagement in change.

We've highlighted the steps and concepts by illustrating them through real examples from companies in various stages of their journeys, as well as evolved cultures that are focused on sustaining excellence. We have seen these cultural transformations actually work, and we have also seen other efforts sub-optimize. We know the key to success is leadership.

We've envisioned culture change as a product of purposefully changing *everything* together—processes, customer focus, collaborative norms, measures, organization, goals, technology, skill, capabilities, and most of all, leadership. Again, that greater strategy looks like Figure 24.

As we've said, a Lean Culture of Engaged Team Performance aligns processes, measures, goals, norms, standards, and organization with customer needs. In order to attain and sustain that alignment, you have to be willing to purposefully change all of those things in concert, and you have to empower your whole team to lead those changes.

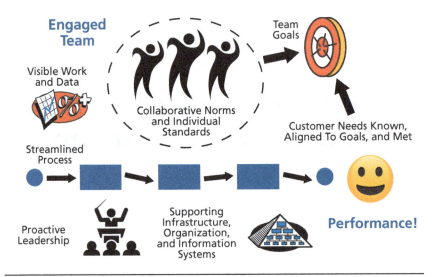

Figure 24 A Lean Culture of Engaged Team Performance.

We've also talked about the steps to transforming your organization to a Lean Culture of Engaged Team Performance. Those steps were:

1. *Commit to change.* Find your inspirational purpose and build a platform for change.
2. *Measure and analyze the process.* Investigate the current process and customer requirements, and measure outcomes and work standards.
3. *Streamline the work.* Improve the flow of the process to deliver value efficiently.
4. *Make the work and data visible.* Make the new work processes, collaborative norms, and control measures visually obvious in the workplace.
5. *Organize the team.* Reorganize and right-size the team for the work.
6. *Set team goals.* Assess team performance and establish team goals.
7. *Lead the transition.* Visionary leadership must invest in the culture, developing the skills, tools, systems, and knowledge to move the team to the envisioned future state.
8. *Sustain Engaged Team Performance.* Demonstrate performance over time.

Hopefully the steps and their linear progression make sense now that you've seen detailed examples of the approach to implementing them. As we've shown, a leader of a small team can use this transformational approach, or a CEO can deploy it across her entire organization. Regardless, get the entire team to participate in the transformation.

Along the way, we've discussed some new twists on the traditional Lean tools that can help you to drive and sustain that transformation:

- Self-reported *Time Studies* to gather critical data about your standard work
- The *Opportunity Matrix* to take a logically-ordered approach to prioritizing different options in streamlining the process
- *Efficiency Charts* to monitor performance opportunities and allow teams to self-manage by clearly seeing the gap between their capacity and their output
- *Customer-Focused Teams* for optimal alignment of process, team, and customer with data-based right-sizing to match capacity to demand
- *Mission 24* to drive a team goal of getting all of the work done without backlog
- *Strategy Deployment* to integrate the Lean concept of Hoshin planning into the portfolio management processes that need to occur in every organization's annual planning cycle

We've also mentioned *Agile* as a special application of Lean Culture with specific processes, measures, and collaborative norms that are designed for software and product development teams. See Appendix B for a description of Agile that highlights Menlo Innovations' unique approach, which combines Lean and team engagement principles in pursuit of joy in a software development environment.

Finally, we'll introduce *Value Innovation,* the topic coming up next, as the guiding principle that sustains and invigorates a Lean Culture by continually renewing the organization's connections to its customers and markets.

The key concept was that all of those tools and ideas are mutually supporting. They are most valuable when deployed all together.

A LEAN CULTURE OF VALUE INNOVATION

After achieving joy in your current culture, the final frontier in evolving and sustaining your Lean Culture will be getting your entire organization truly focused on long-term value innovation.

While an inwardly-focused Lean effort may allow your organization to compete and survive in the short-to-medium term, you'll need to create new innovative solutions in order to deliver enough value for your markets that will allow your organization to thrive over time. A whole new industry is springing up around the need to spark innovation, combining classic brainstorming tools with the idea-generation pipelines of crowd-sourcing, the portfolio management of strategy deployment (introduced earlier), and the focus on measuring and improving the overall customer experience that is now beginning to be called "CX." None of that theory is rocket science, of course, but similar to a number of other concepts that we've illustrated in this book, the power of the new approach is in *combining* those other best practices in a focused way.

Interestingly, the classic Lean story of Toyota is the perfect one for both process streamlining and employee engagement, but the company isn't necessarily considered a dominant force in market innovation today. Decades ago, Toyota used Lean waste reduction and a deep focus on Quality in order to differentiate its products and gain a significant market share, and so in that way, they are certainly an innovative company. But it seems that leadership in innovation comes and goes. Other car companies copied Toyota's approach, with varying success, and some have recently closed the gap in efficiency and quality. As a recent owner of vehicles from Toyota, Audi, and Ford, for example, I've seen better entertainment systems, more intuitive controls, and stronger dealer service with the other brands. I'm not sure yet what kind my next vehicle purchase will be, but I don't see a single obvious choice.

When we bought our Toyota a few years ago, we had to convince one of our young daughters that the brakes would actually work, because even a 10-year-old had heard about the brake and accelerator setbacks that the company had experienced. Even more recently, our environmentally conscious kids have heard about the innovative solution that Volkswagen (parent of Audi) engineers developed to defeat government air quality tests in their not-so-clean-diesel cars. That ethical lapse was an example of innovative thinking gone wild. Ethics matter.

One reason that companies don't sustain innovation leadership may be that they're not really innovating purposefully and embedding innovative thinking into their cultures. Maybe some get lucky with a new product that can drive a decade or two of shareholder value, but that luck is hard to replicate over time without a conscious focus.

A VALUE INNOVATION STRATEGY

W. Chan Kim and Renee Mauborgne wrote the book *Blue Ocean Strategy* in 2005, and although the word "innovation" isn't in the title, their book is really about innovation. They differentiate "value innovation" as a new way of thinking about integrating business strategy and product innovation, explaining that:

> *Instead of focusing on beating the competition, you focus on making the competition irrelevant by creating a leap in value for buyers and your company, thereby opening up new and uncontested market space.*

Innovating should drive both greater buyer value and lower operational cost, which is quite a paradox since those two outcomes don't always seem to go together. Of course, Toyota's success in making high-quality cars cheaply through a focus on Lean is a great example of that kind of value innovation, but their advantage has been worn down over the years as competitors in the automotive industry have copied the Lean approach.

So, even the birthplace of Lean has to find ways to refresh their strategy in order to stay ahead.

One of the examples that Kim and Mauborgne use to illustrate that value–cost paradox comes from Cirque du Soleil. By combining the human talent acts of a circus and the storyline of live theater, the company created a new type of performance art that really isn't exactly circus or theater. It's something new.

Cheaper to deliver than a circus because of the elimination of animal shows and circus stars, but moving upscale by including a themed theater-style production, Cirque du Soleil created a differentiated value for customers for which they could charge a premium ticket price, yet they accomplished that at a cheaper cost than other circus options. Kim and Mauborgne use a new tool called a Strategy Canvas to show those differences. The Strategy Canvas has a list of critical attributes along the bottom, describing both the old market and the new value proposition, and then compares a number of competitors and/or industry groups as separate lines. A paradigm-shifting product like Cirque du Soleil usually has some new attributes, some comparable concepts, and also a reduced emphasis on other legacy features.

Cirque du Soleil's new market looks like Figure 25.

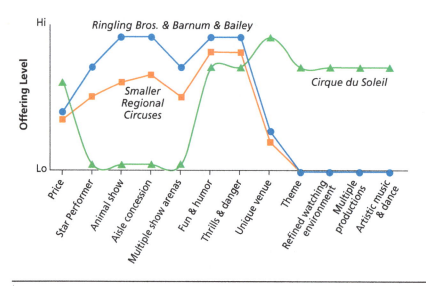

Figure 25 Strategy canvas of Cirque du Soleil, from Blue Ocean Strategy.

The authors of *Blue Ocean Strategy* also traced the consequences for companies that failed to continuously create new value through innovation. For example, Tom Peters highlighted excellent companies over three decades ago in his book, *In Search of Excellence,* and some of those dominating positions were short-lived. Kim and Mauborgne explain:

> *Yet within two years of its publication, a number of the companies surveyed began to slip into oblivion; Atari, Chesebrough-Pond's, Data General, Fluor, National Semiconductor... two-thirds of the identified model firms in the book have fallen from their perches as industry leaders within five years of its publication.*

Some of Peters' excellent companies don't even exist anymore. The world changes, and you have to stay ahead of that change.

Companies without a purposeful innovation strategy will eventually fall behind. Conversely, a value innovation focus enhances your Lean Culture because it orients your team on your customers and potential new customers, reinforcing your purpose for existing in the first place.

Dr. Fred Moll leads Auris Surgical Robotics, a company that is revolutionizing minimally invasive surgery by developing a new generation of robotic medical devices. As a co-founder of four highly successful medical device companies, his motivation for pursuing a career in innovation was centered in a need to keep things interesting, and he has lived the saying, "If you love what you do, you'll never work a day in your life."

> *Life is supposed to be an adventure, and work is a core part of that journey. One of the inherent attributes that makes working in Silicon Valley startups exciting is the shared ownership that motivates the whole organization to function more efficiently. Ownership at every level of the organization creates a shared enthusiasm for success, and people take pride in contributing to a goal larger than themselves. Whether that's in developing a product that creates a better life for someone else or just in knowing that we contributed technology that moved the world forward, everyone on our team likes to think that we've used our time here on earth in a way that's meaningful. At Auris, we believe that what we're trying to accomplish is important, innovative, and will advance the company's value in an exciting way. We each take joy in coming to work every day to contribute something that will change the world for the better.*

Returning to a quote from Rich Sheridan from the Introduction, we now see new meaning in it:

> *Joy is designing and building something that actually sees the light of day and is enjoyably used and widely adopted by the people for whom it was intended... Our mission, which we take very seriously, is to "end human suffering in the world as it relates to technology."*

Menlo Innovations' purpose is directly linked to its innovation strategy. We've now come full circle, and we're back to the beginning of the book, when we built commitment for change in Step 1 by finding your purpose. Once you've found your purpose and designed a Lean Culture to fulfill it, you need to keep feeding it through innovation. While an investment in a Lean Culture can get you to the pinnacle of performance, you have to invest purposefully in innovation to sustain your organization's potential in the long term.

THE FUTURE OF LEAN CULTURE AND ENGAGED TEAM PERFORMANCE

Is employee engagement at the end of the rainbow for you? Or are you trying to get to "joy"?

Rachelle Gagnon of Assumption Life in Canada says, "You won't treat your customers any better than you treat your employees." Her vision doesn't stop at engagement, either. She explains, "Engaging your employees is the buzzword now, but engagement won't be enough in the future. We're already working on *inspiring* our employees."

Recognized as one of the top small and medium sized employers in Canada by Progress 101 and Aon Hewitt, Assumption Life compares the spectrum of employee engagement to the pyramid of Maslow's Hierarchy of Needs, with an Engagement Continuum that begins at satisfaction and aspires to inspiration (see Figure 26).

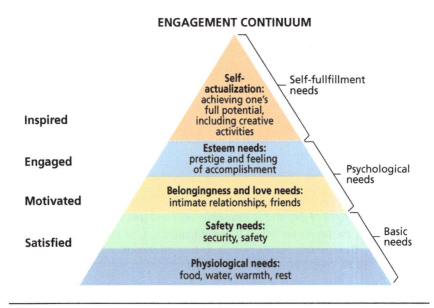

Figure 26 Hierarchy of employee engagement at Assumption Life. (Maslow's Hierarchy from: http://www.21stcentech.com).

Like Gagnon, I believe that simply getting engagement by meeting esteem needs, for example through recognition, won't be enough in the future, and I foresee that self-actualized employees will provide a deep and sustainable competitive advantage for their companies in the long term.

I also believe that the self-actualization at the top of Maslow's pyramid could also be called joy! I hope that you, too, can experience the joy of a Lean Culture of Engaged Team Performance, but you should also recognize that it's a journey, not a destination. You're either improving or you're getting worse, so the work of transforming and sustaining a Lean Culture is never completely done.

Enjoy the journey!

Appendix A
The History of Process and Performance Improvement

We'd like to take a quick look back at the more influential trends and programs that businesses have followed in the modern era.

This appendix will cover the key points of focus over time, emphasizing the swings between production efficiency, quality, sociology, equipment, accounting, processes, and customer satisfaction (see Figure 27). The pendulum of business improvement theory has swung widely and wildly, from precise management of dehumanizing small tasks to culture-based attempts in social engineering; from efficiency to effectiveness; from process focus to customer centricity. Some eras built on what was learned in the previous years, while some apparently were simply reacting to the new conditions they encountered, but all conspired to deliver us here today.

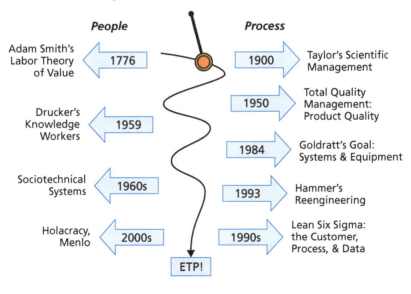

Figure 27 Pendulum swings in business theory.

EARLY IDEAS

Many people think of Henry Ford as the inventor of the car. He wasn't. Ford's contribution was even more substantial: he figured out how to mass produce cars cheaply and quickly, expanding the potential market by making them affordable and available for the vast majority of people. Ford was as much a philosopher as a businessman: his vision for the Model T wasn't just about making money; he wanted to introduce American families to the joy and the freedom of traveling.

So Ford revolutionized the landscape, both figuratively and literally, of the early twentieth century by taking a handcrafted car-manufacturing process and turning it into an assembly line. His original plant made 11 cars in its first month with the old process. A few years later, the same plant was making more than 1,000 cars each month. The new assembly process capitalized on the concept of the *division of labor*, breaking the car-making process into 84 areas that could be learned by different people. By dividing the work into manageable chunks, Ford's process allowed each worker to become an expert in making one part of the car. The assembly line was born.

Ford didn't invent the concept of division of labor. He applied ideas that had been around for decades, including thoughts from Adam Smith, a Scottish economist who had lived a century earlier. Smith saw both positive and negative potential impacts from the predecessors of the assembly line.

Smith believed that division of labor would cause a great increase in production. One example he used was the making of pins: one worker could probably make only twenty pins per day. However, if ten people divided up the eighteen steps required to make a pin, they could make a combined amount of 48,000 pins in one day. However, Smith's views on division of labor are not unambiguously positive, and are typically mischaracterized. In *The Wealth of Nations*, Smith says:

> *In the progress of the division of labour, the employment of the far greater part of those who live by labour, that is, of the great body of the people, comes to be confined to a few very simple operations, frequently only one or two... The man whose whole life is spent in performing a few simple operations, of which the effects too are, perhaps, always the same, or very nearly the same, has no occasion to exert his understanding, or to exercise his invention in finding out expedients for removing difficulties which never occur. He naturally loses, therefore, the habit of such exertion, and generally becomes as stupid and ignorant as it is possible for a human creature to become... this is the state into which the labouring poor, that is, the great body of the people, must necessarily fall, unless government takes some pains to prevent it.*

Smith was a philosopher as well as an economist. Smith was worried that taking the division of labor too far would result in boring, mindless jobs that relegated the poor worker to remain downtrodden forever. Smith wasn't able to envision the vast technological advances that have shifted some of those repetitive roles to machines, so his fears did not fully come to fruition. However, the disparity between rich and poor has continued to increase over time, and jobs have in fact become much more specialized as he foresaw.

As a philosophical aside, consider how that specialization of knowledge has driven our society to become more fragile now compared with Smith's time two centuries ago. Back then, families knew how to do most of the basic things to survive: grow food, make cloth, build a home, and so on. Compare that to our more specialized skills now, and it's obvious that we're more productive as a whole but not as self-sufficient as individuals. The "Hurricane Katrina effect" of societal breakdown after a global natural disaster such as a devastating earthquake or another massive hurricane would actually be worse today than it would have been back then, since most people today would be forced to depend on others for help that might never come. The people of two centuries ago would have just picked up the pieces, rebuilt, and moved on. Unfortunately, as a planet we probably have that challenge coming someday, and it's just a matter of time.

While Henry Ford was designing his first production line, Frederick Winslow Taylor was pioneering the management consulting industry. As described in his book, *The Principles of Scientific Management*, Taylor created four principles of scientific management for the study and control of human work:

1. Replace anecdotal work methods with processes based on a scientific study of the tasks.
2. Proactively select, train, and develop each employee rather than passively leaving the employees to train themselves.
3. Provide detailed instruction for and supervision of each worker in the performance of that worker's specific task.
4. Divide work between managers and workers, so that the managers apply scientific management principles to planning the work and the workers actually perform the tasks.

With the methods and driving influence of people like Taylor, people like Ford applied the concepts of scientific management to enable substantial breakthrough performance improvements from the division of labor. Today almost every process, from applying for a mortgage to going through the buffet line, is somehow modeled after Ford's Model T production line. As we'll see later, some organizations eventually took the assembly-line concept too far, though perhaps without all the evil consequences that Smith feared.

THE EARLY AND MID-TWENTIETH CENTURY

While Taylor was the father of the management consulting industry in the nineteenth century, Peter Drucker became its twentieth-century godfather. Drucker identified some of the key trends in the evolving economy, including the shift toward transactional processes. Today manufacturing is only about 30 percent of the gross domestic product in the United States, and the other 70 percent comes from the service sector. And regardless of whether manufacturing or service, the majority of job roles have transformed to become what Drucker called "knowledge workers" and are the opposite of the mindless roles that Adam Smith feared. The new worker has indispensable skills and knowledge.

Peter Drucker realized that the methods and approaches Taylor created to measure and manage manufacturing work had been thoughtlessly copied and misapplied to knowledge work, and in his book *Management: Tasks, Responsibilities, Practices,* he lamented the lack of follow-through on Taylor's principles:

> *Frederick W. Taylor was the first man in recorded history who deemed work deserving of systematic observation and study. On Taylor's "scientific management" rests, above all, the tremendous surge of affluence in the last seventy-five years which has lifted the working masses in the developed countries well above any level recorded before, even for the well-to-do. Taylor, though the Isaac Newton (or perhaps the Archimedes) of the science of work, laid only first foundations, however. Not much has been added to them since—even though he has been dead all of sixty years.*

Under Drucker's guidance, management consulting took great strides in the later decades of the twentieth century. Visionary thought leaders such as W. Edwards Deming and Joseph Juran led the Total Quality Management movement, while Taiichi Ohno applied the same principles with a slightly different focus in creating the Toyota Production System. But much of the effort was still oriented to improving manufacturing operations, and the transactional and service work again lagged behind.

Managers across the globe enjoyed reading *The Goal,* the book that Eliyahu Goldratt wrote as a fictional story to illustrate the impact of his Theory of Constraints (TOC) on reducing bottlenecks in an assembly line. As organizations became more complex to match their production lines, they applied Goldratt's ideas quite effectively to measure utilization of key *equipment,* while the concept of measuring the effectiveness and productivity of key *people* failed to evolve at the same clip.

SOCIOTECHNICAL SYSTEMS

Sociotechnical Systems (STS) is an approach that focuses on the role of the worker in the workplace in an attempt to find the optimum balance of excellence in technical performance and quality in people's work lives. Coined in the 1960s by Eric Trist and Fred Emery, who were working as consultants at the Tavistock Institute in London, Sociotechnical Systems provide much of the foundation of ETP, even though they were highly theoretical, cumbersome, and time consuming to implement and hence were not widely accepted.

The cornerstone principle of sociotechnical theory is *joint optimization*. In their book *Organizational Choice*, Trist and fellow authors Higgin, Murray, and Pollock explain: "Inherent in the Sociotechnical approach is the notion that the attainment of optimum conditions in any one dimension does not necessarily result in a set of conditions optimum for the system as a whole... The optimization of the whole tends to require a less than optimum state for each separate dimension."

Beginning with an organizational research article based on comparative studies of work crews in British coal mines, where, even as technology was improving, productivity was falling and, even with better pay and amenities, absenteeism was increasing, the theories were evolved into work designs based on the following principles:

- *Responsible autonomy:* Shifting work to teams or groups with internal supervision and leadership, but avoiding the "silo thinking" by studying the whole system

- *Adaptability, agility:* In an environment of increasing complexity, giving these groups responsibility for solving local problems

- *Whole tasks:* Specifying the objective to be completed, with a minimum of regulation of how it is to be done

- *Meaningfulness of tasks:* In the words of Trist et al.: "For each participant the task has total significance and dynamic closure"

Successful implementations of Sociotechnical Systems are relatively few and are either regarded as experiments or carefully shielded from view. Most are "greenfield" (built from the ground up) rather than improvements or transformations of existing plants, and at the time all were based on a tangible product such as coal, coffee, gasoline, paper products, or dog food. Significantly, the Procter & Gamble high-performance plants are on average 35 percent more productive than their traditional counterparts; and although P&G tends to "keep its lamp hidden" and not advertise its differentiators, the company is inundated with requests to benchmark or study the facilities and organizations. As a consequence, P&G is rightfully selective in allowing benchmarking voyages to its facilities.

William Pasmore writes that in spite of the successes, Sociotechnical Systems always faced "stiff resistance from those who preferred the comfort of traditional ways of managing" and "even some successful demonstration projects had shown signs of regression in the face of traditional authoritarianism." It takes a very real change in leadership style to give over control to teams.

ANOTHER SUCCESSFUL TEAM MODEL—W. L. GORE

W. L. Gore created another notable divergence from the mainstream—a company founded in 1958 based on Teflon, with a focus on teams and communication. The company personnel have no ranks and no titles. Anyone can speak to anyone else, and the company is run as a collection of small "task forces" instead of traditional departments. Manufacturing plants have no more than 150 to 200 associates, so that the people all know each other; they can share or tap into knowledge and skills that wouldn't be accessible in a more conventional organization. Team leaders emerge rather than being selected. Unusually high associate satisfaction and retention are attributed to the unusual organizational structure and set of principles.

KAIZEN, WORKOUT, AND REENGINEERING

Kaizen is a much misused word actually meaning "improvement"—not "continuous improvement," as many people think. In Japan, the word is associated with typically small improvements discovered and implemented by the teams of producers who actually do the work. As practiced at Toyota for the last 50 years, the approach is equalizing or egalitarian in nature because people at all levels can participate in eliminating the waste and hard work of production. More recently, Kaizen Events have sprouted up almost everywhere, convening gatherings of process stakeholders for a few hours or a few days to identify issues, offer suggestions, and then hammer out solution plans.

In the early 1990s, GE deployed a successful and popular collaborative problem-solving process, really just a more structured adaptation of Kaizen, called WorkOut. These action-oriented team problem-solving sessions were ideal to bring cross-functional participants together to analyze and resolve simple process issues, and they began to drive great improvements in results for a diverse range of companies. In 1993, Michael Hammer then applied the same holistic process analysis concepts strategically in his book, *Reengineering the Corporation*. Beginning in 1994, Ord Elliott and Implementation Partners refined GE's WorkOut with elements of Reengineering into the Action Forum Process.

The resulting methods, WorkOut, Kaizen, and Reengineering, had the same benefits—speed and action—and the same general weakness: sometimes they tempted people to jump from current state to future state based on process analysis but without appropriate data analysis, which often resulted in unintended consequences. The business improvement landscape was ripe for a more data-based approach.

LEAN AND SIX SIGMA

Consequently, two more major, and at the time competing, disciplines grew out of the melting pot of business-oriented thought in the 1980s and early 1990s. Like WorkOut and Reengineering, Lean and Six Sigma had incorporated time-tested process-based methods for problem solving into their approaches, but they also began to use data in innovative ways to analyze processes before making decisions to change anything.

Lean Enterprise had strong roots from the Toyota Production System of the previous 40 years, and its name actually came from the book called *Lean Thinking* that James Womack and Daniel Jones wrote in 1996 as a sequel to their 1990 book about Toyota, *The Machine That Changed the World*. The Lean approach has probably contributed more than anything else to productivity improvement in the years since.

Womack and Jones explain in *Lean Thinking* that the Lean approach "provides a way to specify value, line up value-creating actions in the best sequence, conduct these activities without interruption whenever someone requests them, and perform them more and more effectively. In short, lean thinking is *lean* because it provides a way to do more and more with less and less—less human effort, less equipment, less time, and less space—while coming closer and closer to providing customers with exactly what they want." Lean in its pure form as Womack and Jones described it in their books definitely has team engagement and human performance components, while most imitators seem to have focused mostly on the process theories rather than leveraging the people aspects. Interestingly, the original Lean theories were quite effective in demonstrating a vision for a better process and organization, but the methodology was not quite so robust in explaining exactly how to make the right "leap" from current to future state.

Six Sigma began in 1987 at Motorola as a product design quality effort and was then transformed by General Electric into a more holistic business improvement system in the decade of the 1990s. *The Six Sigma Way* explained the wild success of GE's approach and popularized the Six Sigma brand name. The Six Sigma approach was really the first integration of quality, root cause, and process improvement principles to incorporate a "simple" five-step execution process, and the book became a cookbook for the thousands of people who were trained to lead the process improvement wave of the future, given mythical belts of various colors, and set loose upon their companies and later the job market.

The last decade has mostly seen enhancements to the two major approaches, most significantly the combination of Lean and Six Sigma (as well as other lesser-known competing methodologies) and the transformation of the methods to apply to transactional and service processes just as well as manufacturing. Lean Six Sigma techniques are still being taught and practiced across the world, generally to positive acclaim and results.

CENTERING THE PENDULUM

And in all that flurry of business process improvement work, a couple of great ideas came along a little too soon and got trumped by the sexier brand names of Lean and Six Sigma. In 1992, Jack Stack wrote *The Great Game of Business* to explain the value of open-book management. His simple yet radical premise was that rather than telling employees only what they "need to know" to do their jobs, management should make the entire business transparent to the whole team. As the president and CEO of the Springfield Remanufacturing Corporation, Stack turned his company around by treating the success of the business as a game and sharing all the results—the numbers—with his entire team. Rather than keeping business performance a secret, he got engaged buy-in from his workforce by showing everyone the truth.

While Stack shared strategic performance information with his employees, James Belasco and Ralph Stayer followed in 1993 with a more tactical approach for engaging people in the business. Their book, *Flight of the Buffalo*, encouraged managers to think differently about their roles. Instead of engaging employees, managers sometimes unintentionally constrict their teams' ability to get work done. Their conclusion was that leaders need to be proactive instead of reactive:

> *I told my people to stop sending me all those reports and data, and instead list the decisions they thought they should be making and could make without consulting me. When the list wasn't long enough, I challenged them to rethink it. I started sending back memos unread and asked the data processing department to take my name off many distribution lists.*
>
> *My change disturbed some people at first. They had difficulty making the shift. With coaching, they finally got the message. Leadership isn't processing papers. It's about making things happen.... The leader encourages people to take self-directed actions to achieve great performance and remove obstacles that stand in their path.*

These two books about employee engagement actually started the process improvement journey for me. In 1997, a division vice president at Coors Brewing Company handed junior leaders in his organization copies of both books and asked us to apply the concepts. I had a hard time looking in the mirror the next day. I was one of those leaders who carried around a clipboard with a list of action items, busily writing down and prioritizing problems. Every time the members of my team encountered an issue, they were well trained to immediately report it to me instead of fixing it. I was enabling the problems instead of the solutions.

At the time, my job was to supervise a beer packaging line, and my team had encountered a productivity problem. Our production numbers had been consistently falling in the last few months, and we were right below the "volume goal" that the company had set for our manufacturing line. So I went into my next team meeting and surprised them: I showed the team the numbers on our recent performance, and I said, "I'm now going to leave the room for an hour, and when I come back, I'd like to see a list of causes of the issues, a list of solutions that you, the team, are going to implement, and a list of things you need from me." I walked out.

When I came back, their list was full, and mine was empty. They implemented solutions such as "rotational coverage of equipment by senior specialists to check machine setups" that allowed the most experienced team members to visit each of the team's machines every day. If I had suggested that solution, I probably would have received a grievance form for breaking departmental seniority work practices; but because it was their own idea, nobody thought to challenge it. The numbers quickly jumped back up into the acceptable range, and I never had to fix anything there again. I just made sure the members of the team knew how we were doing, and I stayed out of their way.

ENGAGED TEAM PERFORMANCE, MENLO, AND HOLACRACY

As some of the experiments in organizational design from Sociotechnical Systems, self-managed teams, and other culture-focused ideas began to show results, people (such as Rich Sheridan at Menlo Innovations in 2001) decided to intentionally deploy culture-based organizational designs as they launched their own companies, many with great success.

Other companies have used the Engaged Team Performance (ETP) approach to improve process and performance in existing cultures. We've been privileged to work with and share stories of companies such as Principal Financial, which spawned the core case study of our prior book, *Building Engaged Team Performance* (McGraw-Hill, 2010).

While each company's journey is different in some ways, the common threads are explained in this book. Following the eight-step ETP deployment approach helps. Generally, each culture has to create a set of "collaborative norms" (commonly-agreed ways of people working together) and enforce self-discipline that comes from within the team instead of imposing top-down discipline from the leader.

As some of those cultures matured, people named them and tried to market them. One recent example is the concept of "Holacracy" mentioned in this book in discussions of Zappos.com. Holacracy didn't actually begin at Zappos. According to Wikipedia:

> *Holacracy is a specific social technology or system of organizational governance… in which authority and decision-making are distributed throughout a holarchy of self-organizing teams rather than being vested in a management hierarchy. Holacracy has been adopted in for-profit and non-profit organizations in Australia, France, Germany, New Zealand, Switzerland, the United Kingdom, and the United States.*
>
> *The term holacracy is derived from the term holarchy, coined by Arthur Koestler in his 1967 book* The Ghost in the Machine. *A holarchy is composed of holons (Greek for "whole") or units that are autonomous and self-reliant, but also dependent on the greater whole of which they are part. Thus a holarchy is a hierarchy of self-regulating holons that function both as autonomous wholes and as dependent parts.*

In practice, holarchy creates circles of self-managed teams to replace the traditional triangles of leadership hierarchy. While some might compare that instead to *anarchy*, the approach actually requires more collaboration and self-discipline from everyone. Leadership becomes everyone's responsibility, and team management functions such as hiring and performance feedback are shared. Some people don't fit well in that kind of environment, and they often self-select out.

SUMMARY

We hope you've been able to hang in here for the history and philosophy lesson, because the past helps explain the gaps in the current state of the business and consulting thought process. In short, people have studied the technical side of work and process improvement for more than a hundred years, and we've glossed over equally important work about the psychology of the human worker. With knowledge workers now forming the majority of the economy, the combination of technical analysis methods with human teamwork and motivation approaches has been haphazard at best, and counterproductive at worst.

This Appendix was all about forming the appropriate combination of the technical and human sides of work, integrating process with performance. As you've seen, each side holds a key part of the opportunity. Both sides are critical and have to be considered together.

Hope the history helps!

Appendix B
The Joy of Agile Product Development

We have introduced thoughts from Richard Sheridan in many of this book's chapters, recounting the intentional culture of engaged team performance at Menlo Innovations that Sheridan recently documented in his book, *Joy Inc.* I've toured his company's facility and have seen it with my own eyes.

It's definitely different. It's also brilliant.

Their culture works because it is intentionally designed that way.

AGILE

First of all, their work processes are Agile. In fact, these folks were Agile before Agile was cool.

Agile is a system of flexible project management that is becoming quite popular today, mostly in software design functions, but that popularity is expanding to include other types of innovative product development. Our company has recently done Agile transformations with teams that make everything from dental plans and life insurance policies to medical robots and jet engines, so the concepts are useful much more broadly than just in software. But Agile's special adaptation of Lean Culture principles fits very well for software development work, where the main idea is to avoid non-value-added rework by developing the product in rapidly iterating layers.

Iterative software development goes all the way back to 1957, and the seeds of the Agile methodology were sown over decades, culminating in a meeting in February 2001, where 17 software developers from different organizations met to discuss new development methods. They then published the *Manifesto for Agile Software Development* (available at: http://www.agilemanifesto.org/principles.html) in which they said that by uncovering better ways of developing software by doing it and helping others do it, they have come to value *individuals and interactions* over processes and tools, *working software* over comprehensive documentation, *customer collaboration* over contract negotiation, and *responding to change* over following a plan.

Introducing the Agile Manifesto on behalf of the Agile Alliance, Jim Highsmith said:

> *The Agile movement is not anti-methodology, in fact many of us want to restore credibility to the word methodology. We want to restore a balance. We embrace modeling, but not in order to file some diagram in a dusty corporate repository. We embrace documentation, but not hundreds of pages of never-maintained and rarely-used tomes. We plan, but recognize the limits of planning in a turbulent environment. Those who would brand proponents of XP or SCRUM or any of the other Agile Methodologies as "hackers" are ignorant of both the methodologies and the original definition of the term hacker.*

It was another revolution.

AGILE PRINCIPLES

Again referencing the useful summary that you can find at agilemanifesto.org, the Agile Manifesto is based on twelve principles:

1. Customer satisfaction by early and continuous delivery of valuable software.
2. Welcome changing requirements, even in late development.
3. Working software is delivered frequently (weeks rather than months).
4. Close, daily cooperation between business people and developers.
5. Projects are built around motivated individuals, who should be trusted.
6. Face-to-face conversation is the best form of communication (co-location).
7. Working software is the principal measure of progress.
8. Sustainable development, able to maintain a constant pace.
9. Continuous attention to technical excellence and good design.

10. Simplicity—the art of maximizing the amount of work not done—is essential.
11. Best architectures, requirements, and designs emerge from self-organizing teams.
12. Regularly, the team reflects on how to become more effective, and adjusts accordingly.

While expressed above just in terms of software design, the Agile approach aligns very well with the broader concepts of Lean Engaged Team Performance that we've already illustrated, specifically:

Processes:

The calendar is aligned with regular "sprints" of work (often in two-week cycles, but we sometimes see four-week or other variants), each with a cycle of kickoff planning, execution, demonstration ("demo"—a real "show and tell" of the product features that got developed), and a team retrospective ("retro") on how to improve their own work. All of the potential work that the team could do is prioritized in a "backlog." In this case backlog is a good thing, because it allows the team to decide, with real customer input, which features are most important to develop first instead of trying to make the product do everything and taking forever to build it.

Measurement:

Agile teams estimate work at a finite level, breaking features that need development into a multitude of "stories" (each with a customer focus), then estimating the work effort to create each one. That estimation becomes accurate as teams get better at doing it, allowing strong prediction of work effort comparable to the standard time concept that we discussed in previous chapters. The team will then use a "burndown chart" to monitor progress toward completion of all of the work at the end of the two-week cycle, comparing the amount of work remaining to the amount of time the team has left.

Visual Work and Data:

Using manual whiteboards similar to the ones we described in previous chapters, but also integrating software and display screens that are tailored to track and manage each story though the development process, the team always knows exactly where they are, what has been done, and what needs to get done next.

Collaborative Norms:

Agile teams do daily huddles called "scrums." In rugby, the team moves the ball down the field together as one unit, interchanging roles as needed to get the job done. The word "scrum" visualizes the concept of an engaged work team that collaborates to win.

Organization:

Unlike some other product development situations where the work might be a part-time role for some, Agile deploys small five- to nine-person dedicated teams that continuously work together on the development effort. The organization scales by cloning and adding teams, not by making existing teams larger. As we've discussed, executing that team concept requires substantial cross-training and dedication to allowing each individual to learn and grow.

Culture:

Teams love Agile. It feels great to get something done every two weeks instead of waiting a year to see if the code passes testing. People get to develop new skills by cross-training. While they live in a very flexible workplace, they also have to exhibit great self-discipline and collaboration in following the process.

The flow of a two-week Agile sprint looks like Figure 28.

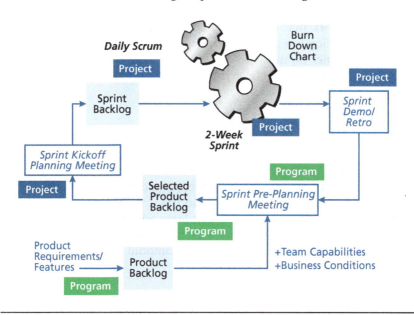

Figure 28 Agile sprint cycle.

You may notice in the diagram above that there are two levels of teams shown. A "scaled Agile framework" of multiple project teams working on a larger development effort will require a *program level* prioritization of backlog prior to assigning two weeks' worth of work to each scrum team for each cycle. Representatives of each project team work with customers to form the program team, then facilitate their own *project level* teams in executing work.

LEADING TO JOY: A PURPOSEFUL CULTURE

So a person familiar with Agile and Lean and touring the Menlo Innovations facility would see Agile and Lean principles everywhere.

But the culture at Menlo Innovations goes far beyond the processes and collaborative norms of Agile project management. While their work processes are inherently Agile, Menlo's version takes it to an even purer form, which the team has perfected over two decades and includes:

- Faster one-week cycles of the "sprint" iterative development concept.

- Tracking "actual actuals" of time it took to do each task, but only for the purpose of planning better the next time, not for holding individuals accountable to work harder (which, as Sheridan says, would just result in padded estimates in the future, like many other companies have).

- Paired programming, with two developers working on one keyboard, and other collaborative norms such as tracking project status with cards and yarn that you'd have to see to believe.

- A culture that celebrates people, who along with their dogs and babies on their work floor every day, make hiring and promotion decisions, take leadership roles intuitively when something needs to get done, and take joy in their work.

Do you see joy at your workplace every day? I could go on and on about Menlo, but if you're interested you should probably just read Sheridan's book, *Joy, Inc.*, or go see it for yourself. They give tours any time someone shows up.

Seeing Menlo will help you realize that *you can make your culture into anything you want it to be, as long as you do that purposefully.* How can you do that? Here are two guiding questions:

1. Do you have a product development team that creates new products or services for your organization? Is there an opportunity to apply the special tools of Agile Development there in support of your Lean Culture transformation?

2. Are you brave enough to change your purpose, as Menlo Innovations has done, to orient on creating a joyful work environment for the benefit of both your customers and your employees? Do you believe yet in the business value of joy?

Go for it!

Inspirational Sources

While the text references a number of other sources directly as well, I'd recommend reading the books below for their important contributions to the thoughts within *The Joy of Lean*:

Belasco, James A. and Ralph C. Stayer. *Flight of the Buffalo,* Warner Books, 1993.

Dweck, Carol S. *Mindset,* Ballantine Books, 2006.

Marquet, L. David. *Turn the Ship Around!* Penguin Group, 2012.

Sheridan, Richard. *Joy, Inc.,* Penguin Group, 2013.

Stack, Jack. *The Great Game of Business,* Crown Business, 1992.

Starbird, Dodd and Roland Cavanagh. *Building Engaged Team Performance,* McGraw-Hill, 2010.

Wheeler, Donald. *Understanding Variation,* SPC Press, 2000.

Index

A
abandon rates, 57
account closure payment process, 43–48, *45f, 47f*
"actual actuals," 145
adherence, defined, 55
Agile product development, 6, 109, 121, 141–145
Agile sprint cycle, *144f*
annual performance reviews, 86–87
assembly line revolution, 48–49
Assumption Life, 6, 126
Auris Surgical Robotics, 124
available production time, 88–92
average speed of answer (ASA), 55, 57

B
backlogs, 81–82, 107
"band and brand" analogies, 110–111
Belasco, James, 136
Blue Ocean Strategy (Kim and Mauborgne), 123, 124
Bono, 110–111
Building Engaged Team Performance (Starbird and Cavanagh), 1, 11, 34, 67, 87, 97, 137
business value of joy, 5–6

C
capacity, 84–85
capacity change, opportunity for, 88–92
Chamberlain, Joshua L., 98–100, 102
change
 challenges of, 20
 commitment to, 14–15
 finding purpose for, 15–18

change resistance
 circles and triangles, 101
 downhill battles, 98–100
 leading engagement, 102–103
 rebellion or revolution, 100–101
 uphill battles, 97–98
cheap labor, 11
cherry-credit, 94
cherry-picking jobs, 94
Cirque du Soleil, 123, *124f*
Clayton, Adam, 110–111
Cline, David, 74, 112
collaborative norms, 62–64, 81, 144
communication, 110–111
Confederate Army example, 98–100
contact center pressure, 55–57
Coors Brewing Company, 52, 59–62, 137
cost of poor culture, 5–6
cost of poor quality, 38, 40
cross-training, 76, 81, 83
culture, sheep dip training and, 2–3
culture change, negative to positive, 94
culture crash, 106–107
culture design, purposeful, 5–6
culture of excellence, 1
culture paradox, 10–11
Culture That Rocks (Knight), 110–111

D
daily scrums, *144f*
Deming, W. Edwards, 87
differential credit, 94
dog-walking example, 49–50
downhill battles, 98–100
Drucker, Peter, 3
Dweck, Carol, 12, 86

E

Ecova, Inc., 13–14, 20–21, 65, 69–70, 72, 112–116
efficiency charts, 88–92, 89f, 91f, 94–95
efficiency improvement, 11
efficient work, 11
employee engagement, 6
empowerment, 7–8, 110
Engaged Team Performance (ETP) theories, 48
engagement, 6, 8–9, 102–103
engagement continuum, 126f
"Everybody's Jumping on the Lean Bandwagon" (Pay), 1–2
EZB (easy to do business), 43–48

F

feedback, 88–92
5S: workplace organization, 51–52
fixed-mindset people, 12
flex work, 54–57
Flight of the Buffalo (Belasco and Stayer), 136
Ford, Henry, 48
freedom through tyranny, 66–67
Friedrich, Amy, 50
frozen middle, 20

G

Gagnon, Rachelle, 6, 126
"gamification," 68
Gettysburg, Battle of, 98–100
goal setting, 95–96
Grand Paradox of an Efficient Culture, 10–11
The Great Game of Business (Stack), 59, 136
growth-mindset people, 12

H

hand offs, 48–51, 81
Highsmith, Jim, 142
Holacracy, 101, 102, 138
Hoshin Planning, 113
"How Going Lean Saved These Companies" (Tetford), 10–11
Hsieh, Tony, 102

I

individual goals, 81, 85–87, 94
Industry Week survey (2007), 1–2
"island of Lean Culture," 108

J

Jones, Daniel, 1
Joppa (non-profit), 16
Joy, Inc. (Sheridan), 5–6, 22, 66, 71, 100–101, 125

K

Kaipa, Prasad, 15
Kaizen events, 52
Kim, W. Chan, 123, 124
Kirkley, Lauren, 115
Knight, Jim, 86, 110–111
Koestler, Arthur, 138

L

leader involvement, 110
leader standard work, 112–115
leadership, essential nature of, 1, 21, 22, 106–107
Lean
  cultural components of, 2–3
  as empowerment, 7
  and Engaged Team Performance (ETP) theories, 48
  history of, 3–4
  spirit of, 48–51
  Wikipedia summary of, 4
Lean Culture of Engaged Team Performance, 3f, 120f
  alignment with customer needs, 3
  benefits for leaders, 67
  communication, 110–111
  culture crash, 106–108
  empowerment, 110
  expansion of, 112
  future of, 126–127
  as intentional journey, 119
  leadership, 101, 105–107, 110, 116–117
  morale and, 10
  paradox, 10–11, 105–106
  process-only focus, 105–106
  resources, 109
  steps to achieve, 11, 120
  strategy deployment, sustainment of, 115–116
  strategy deployment and standard work, 112–115
  sustainable transformation, 108–112
  time requirements, 109
  tools, 121
  training, 109
  transformation challenges, 97–103
  Value Innovation, 122–125

Index

Lean leadership, 12, 101, 105–107, 110, 116–117
Lean Office and Service Simplified (Locher), 16
Lean parable, xv–xvii
Lean Process Streamlining
   5S: workplace organization, 51–52
   contact center pressure, 55
   EZB, 43–48
   flex work and, 54–57
   Opportunity Matrix, 52–54, *53f*
   process streamlining, 57–59
   spirit of Lean, 48–51
   useful questions, 58
Lean Thinking (Womack and Jones), 1
Liker, Jeffrey, 2
line of sight to the customer, 10, 71, 77, 95
Locher, Drew, 16

M

Machiavelli, Niccolo, 57
Manifesto for Agile Software Development, 141
Marquet, David, 7, 68, 116
Maslow's Hierarchy of Needs, 126
Mauborgne, Renee, 123, 124
Menlo Innovations, 5–6, 86–87, 125, 141–145
merit ratings, 87
Mindset (Dweck), 12, 86
Mission 24, 82–84, *83f*
Moll, Fred, 124–125
morale, team, 10
motivation, 84–85
Mullen, Larry Jr., 110–111
Mulligan, Christopher, 6

N

negative culture improvement, 94–95
negative feelings, 94
negative peer pressure, 94

O

opportunity for capacity change, 88–92
opportunity for improvement
   commitment, 23
   need for change, 23
   path to improvement, 23–24
   process measurement and analysis, 40–41
   quality, 37–40
   results, 24–25
   time study, need for, 25–31
   time study results, 32–37
   transition, 24
Opportunity Matrix, 52–54, *53f*
organizational design, benefits of, 75
Out of the Crisis (Deming), 87
over staffing, 92

P

pacing work, 94
paired programming, 145
Pay, Rick, 2
perfection, vision of, 18–19
performance efficiency, 34–37, *36f*
performance reviews, 86–87
performance standards, 87
Peters, Tom, 124
pilot projects, 74–75, 101
positive peer pressure, 95
The Prince (Machiavelli), 57
Principal Financial, 1, 54, 81
process and performance improvement history, *129f*
   Coors Brewing Company, 137
   early ideas, 130–131
   Flight of the Buffalo (Belasco and Stayer), 136
   The Great Game of Business (Stack), 136
   Holacracy, 138
   Kaizen, WorkOut, and Reengineering, 134–135
   Lean and Six Sigma, 135–136
   Menlo Innovations, 137–138
   sociotechnical systems, 133–134
   twentieth century, 132
   W.L. Gore, 134
   Zappos.com, 138
process change, challenge of, 48
process excellence, 1
process measurement and analysis, 40–41
process streamlining, 43–48, 57–59
process-only focus, 105–106
productivity goals, 84–85, 87, 88–92
productivity measurement, 87–92
purpose, for change, 15–18
purpose, leadership and, 22

Q

quality principles, 39–40

R

rebellion phase of transformation, 100–101
reorganization, fear of, 77–78
resource requirements, 109
Restwell Mattresses, 10–11
rewards and recognition, 8
Roche, 17
role differentiation, 81
Rother, Mike, 2
Rucker, Darius, 15

S

saving completions, 94
Schmidt, Jana, 13–14, 20–21, 112
"scrums," 143
sheep dip training, 2–3
Sheridan, Rich, 5–6, 22, 66, 71, 86–87, 100–101, 125, 137–138, 141–145
Shingo Prize committee, 2
single-piece flow, 48–49
Southwest Airlines, 5
"Special Cause and Common Cause" variation, 65
"sprint" interative development cycles, 145
Stack, Jack, 59, 68, 136
standard time per task, 34, 88–92, 94–95
standard work, 112–115
Stayer, Ralph, 136
stealing work, 93
strategy deployment, 112–116, *114f*
Strug, Kerri, 9
Summer Olympics, 8–9
sustainable transformation, 108–112

T

TalentKeepers, Inc., 6
team goals
 basketball legends and, 86
 customer needs and, 95
 feedback, 88
 individual goals, 85–87
 leadership issues, 95–96
 measuring productivity, 87–92
 Mission 24, 82–84
 negative culture improvement, 94–95
 productivity goals, 84–85
 right sizing, 83
 stealing work, 93
teams
 Agile product development, 141–145
 customer-focused, 71–72
 functional organization, 69–70
 mission, 81–82
 power of, 8–9
 right sizing, 84–85, 88, 92–96
Tetford, Bob, 10–11
time requirements, 109
time studies
 client management task time, 33
 design of, 26–31
 need for, 25–26
 performance efficiency, 34–37
 results, 32–37
 standard time per task, 34
Toyota, Lean and, 3, 52, 122
training, as enabler of strategy, 2–3
training requirements, 109
trend charts, 65–66
Turn the Ship Around! (Marquet), 7, 68

U

U2 (band), 110–111
Understanding Variation (Wheeler), 65
uphill battles, 97–98

V

Value Innovation, 122–125
value–cost paradox, 123
variation, task, 94
vision of perfection, 18–19
visual work and data
 Agile product development, 143
 collaborative norms, 62–64
 at Coors Brewing Company, 59–62
 department organization, 75–77
 freedom through tyranny, 66–67
 leading the process and next steps, 67–68
 pilots, 74–75
 team leadership, 77–79
 trend charts, 65–66
 whiteboard use, 60–62, *60f*, 64–65

W–Y

wastes
 eight classic, 4–5, 44
 suggested ninth, 5
Welch, Jack, 21
Wheeler, Donald, 65
whiteboards, 60–62, *60f*, 64–65, 83, 107
"Why Lean Programs Fail" (Liker and Rother), 2

"Why Measuring Efficiency is Anti-Lean," 95
Wilson, Jennifer, 20–21, 65, 70–71, 76–77
Womack, James, 1
Wooden, John, 86
work completion time credit, 88–92
workplace organization (5S), 51–52

Z

Zander, Ed, 15
Zappos.com, 5, 101, 102, 138

The Knowledge Center
www.asq.org/knowledge-center

Learn about quality. Apply it. Share it.

ASQ's online Knowledge Center is the place to:

- Stay on top of the latest in quality with Editor's Picks and Hot Topics.
- Search ASQ's collection of articles, books, tools, training, and more.
- Connect with ASQ staff for personalized help hunting down the knowledge you need, the networking opportunities that will keep your career and organization moving forward, and the publishing opportunities that are the best fit for you.

Use the Knowledge Center Search to quickly sort through hundreds of books, articles, and other software-related publications.

www.asq.org/knowledge-center

Ask a Librarian

Did you know?

- The ASQ Quality Information Center contains a wealth of knowledge and information available to ASQ members and non-members

- A librarian is available to answer research requests using ASQ's ever-expanding library of relevant, credible quality resources, including journals, conference proceedings, case studies and Quality Press publications

- ASQ members receive free internal information searches and reduced rates for article purchases

- You can also contact the Quality Information Center to request permission to reuse or reprint ASQ copyrighted material, including journal articles and book excerpts

- For more information or to submit a question, visit **http://asq.org/knowledge-center/ask-a-librarian-index**

Visit www.asq.org/qic for more information.

TRAINING   CERTIFICATION   CONFERENCES   MEMBERSHIP   **PUBLICATIONS**

Belong to the Quality Community!

Established in 1946, ASQ is a global community of quality experts in all fields and industries. ASQ is dedicated to the promotion and advancement of quality tools, principles, and practices in the workplace and in the community.

The Society also serves as an advocate for quality. Its members have informed and advised the U.S. Congress, government agencies, state legislatures, and other groups and individuals worldwide on quality-related topics.

Vision

By making quality a global priority, an organizational imperative, and a personal ethic, ASQ becomes the community of choice for everyone who seeks quality technology, concepts, or tools to improve themselves and their world.

ASQ is...

- More than 90,000 individuals and 700 companies in more than 100 countries

- The world's largest organization dedicated to promoting quality

- A community of professionals striving to bring quality to their work and their lives

- The administrator of the Malcolm Baldrige National Quality Award

- A supporter of quality in all sectors including manufacturing, service, healthcare, government, and education

- YOU

Visit www.asq.org for more information.

TRAINING   CERTIFICATION   CONFERENCES   MEMBERSHIP   **PUBLICATIONS**

ASQ Membership

Research shows that people who join associations experience increased job satisfaction, earn more, and are generally happier*. ASQ membership can help you achieve this while providing the tools you need to be successful in your industry and to distinguish yourself from your competition. So why wouldn't you want to be a part of ASQ?

Networking

Have the opportunity to meet, communicate, and collaborate with your peers within the quality community through conferences and local ASQ section meetings, ASQ forums or divisions, ASQ Communities of Quality discussion boards, and more.

Professional Development

Access a wide variety of professional development tools such as books, training, and certifications at a discounted price. Also, ASQ certifications and the ASQ Career Center help enhance your quality knowledge and take your career to the next level.

Solutions

Find answers to all your quality problems, big and small, with ASQ's Knowledge Center, mentoring program, various e-newsletters, *Quality Progress* magazine, and industry-specific products.

Access to Information

Learn classic and current quality principles and theories in ASQ's Quality Information Center (QIC), *ASQ Weekly* e-newsletter, and product offerings.

Advocacy Programs

ASQ helps create a better community, government, and world through initiatives that include social responsibility, Washington advocacy, and Community Good Works.

Visit www.asq.org/membership for more information on ASQ membership.

*2008, The William E. Smith Institute for Association Research

TRAINING CERTIFICATION CONFERENCES MEMBERSHIP **PUBLICATIONS**